Step-By-Step

50 Best-Ever Barbecues

STEP-BY-STEP

50 Best-Ever Barbecues

Christine France

Photographs by Don Last

Acropolis
Books

First published in 1996 by Lorenz Books

© 1996 Anness Publishing Limited

Lorenz Books is an imprint of
Anness Publishing Limited
Boundary Row Studios
1 Boundary Row
London SE1 8HP

ISBN 1 85967 169 1

A CIP catalogue record is available from the British Library

Publisher: Joanna Lorenz
Project Editor: Joanne Rippin
Designer: Adrian Morris
Photographer: Don Last
Stylist: Fiona Tillet

MEASUREMENTS
Three sets of equivalent measurements have been provided in the recipes here, in the following
order: Metric, Imperial and American. It is essential that units of measurement are not mixed
within each recipe. Where conversions result in awkward numbers, these have been rounded
for convenience, but are accurate enough to produce successful results.

CONTENTS

Introduction   6

MEAT   22

POULTRY AND GAME   40

FISH AND SEAFOOD   52

VEGETABLES AND VEGETARIAN DISHES   68

DESSERTS   84

Index   96

INTRODUCTION

However simple the food, there's something about the char-grilled flavour of barbecued food that makes it taste extra-special. Maybe it's also the fresh air that sharpens the appetite and makes that tantalizing aroma so totally irresistible.

There's nothing new about cooking over charcoal; in fact, it's a method of cooking that has been used in most civilizations throughout history. Little has changed about the basic method over the centuries, but many modern barbecues are very sophisticated, making the job easier, cleaner and more controllable. Whether you're cooking over a simple pile of sticks, or on a top-of-the-range barbecue, outdoor cooking can be fun, easy and inexpensive.

There are disputes over the origin of the word barbecue, but one explanation is that it comes from *barbacoa*, an American-Spanish word used by the Arawak Indians of the Caribbean, as the name for the wooden frame that held their food over an open fire as it cooked. The Arawak Indians were cannibals, so the food we cook today is, thankfully, rather different from their offerings!

Whatever your tastes, this collection of recipes offers new, unusual ideas for your barbecue as well as the traditional favourites. There's something for every occasion, from family meals to entertaining: spicy, fruity and exotic grills with fish, meat and poultry; easy sauces, marinades and glazes; and luscious puddings for the sweet-toothed. Vegetarians need not feel left out as there's a whole chapter of simple, tasty vegetarian ideas too.

Best of all, not only does a barbecue set the cook free from the kitchen but, for once, everyone else actually wants to help with the cooking!

Choosing a Barbecue

There is a huge choice of ready-made barbecues on the market and it's important to choose one that suits your needs. First decide how many people you usually cook for and where you are likely to use the barbecue. For instance, do you usually have barbecues just for the family, or are you likely to have barbecue parties for lots of friends? Once you've decided on your basic requirements, you will be able to choose between the different types more easily.

Hibachi Barbecues
These small cast-iron barbecues originated in Japan – the word hibachi translates literally as "firebox". They are inexpensive, easy to use and transportable. Lightweight versions are now made in steel or aluminium.

Disposable Barbecues
These will last for about an hour, and are a convenient idea for picnic-style barbecues, or for cooking just a few small pieces of food.

Portable Barbecues
These are usually quite light and fold away to fit into a car boot so you can take them on picnics. Some are even small enough to fit in a rucksack.

Brazier Barbecues
These open barbecues are suitable for use on a patio or in the garden. Most have legs or wheels and it's a good idea to check that the height suits you. The grill area varies in size and the barbecue may be round or rectangular. It's useful to choose one that has a shelf attached to the side. Other extras may include an electric, battery or clockwork spit: choose one on which you can adjust the height of the spit. Many have a hood, which is useful for a windbreak and gives a place to mount the spit.

Permanent Barbecues

These are a good idea if you often have barbecues at home and can be built simply and cheaply. Choose a sheltered site that is a little way from the house, but with easy access to the kitchen. Permanent barbecues can be built with ordinary household bricks, but it's best to line the inside with firebricks, which will withstand the heat better. Use a metal shelf for the fuel and a grid at whatever height you choose. Packs containing all you need to build a barbecue are available.

Kettle-Grill Barbecues

These have a large, hinged lid which can be used as a windbreak; when closed, the lid lets you use the barbecue rather like an oven. Even large joints of meat or whole turkeys cook very successfully, as the heat reflected within the dome helps to brown the meat evenly. The heat is easily controlled by the use of efficient air vents. This type of barbecue can also be used for home-smoking foods.

Gas Barbecues

The main advantage of these is their convenience – the heat is instant and easily controllable. The disadvantage is that they tend to be quite expensive.

Improvized Barbecues

The most basic barbecues can be built at no cost at all. A pile of stones topped with chicken wire and fuelled with driftwood or kindling, makes a very efficient barbecue. Or, find a large biscuit tin and punch a few holes in it; fill it with charcoal and place a grid on top.

Types of Fuel

If you have a gas or electric barbecue, you will not need to buy extra fuel, but most other barbecues use charcoal or wood. Whatever type of barbecue you have, choose good-quality fuel, and always store it in a dry place.

Woodchips or Herbs
These are designed to be added to the fire to impart a pleasant aroma to the food. They can be soaked, to make them last longer. Scatter them straight on to the coals during cooking, or place them on a metal tray under the grill rack. Packs of hickory or oak chips are easily available, or you can simply scatter twigs of juniper, rosemary, thyme, sage or fennel over the fire.

Lumpwood Charcoal
This is usually made from softwood, and comes in lumps of varying size. It is easier to ignite than briquettes, but tends to burn up faster. Self-igniting Charcoal is simply lumpwood charcoal or briquettes, treated with a flammable substance that catches light very easily. It's important to wait until the ignition agent has burnt off before cooking food, or the smell may taint the food.

Coconut-shell Charcoal
This is not widely available, but makes a good fuel for small barbecues. It's best used on a fire grate with small holes, as the small pieces tend to fall through the gaps.

Charcoal Briquettes
These burn for a long time with the minimum of smell and smoke. They can take time to ignite, however.

Wood
Hardwoods such as oak, apple, olive and cherry are best for barbecues, as they burn slowly with a pleasant aroma. Softwoods, however, tend to burn too fast and give off sparks and smoke, so they are unsuitable for most barbecues. Wood fires need constant attention to achieve an even and steady heat.

Safety Tips

Barbecueing is a perfectly safe method of cooking if it's done sensibly – use these simple guidelines as a basic checklist to safeguard against accidents. If you have never organized a barbecue before, keep your first few events as simple as possible with just one or two types of food. When you have mastered the technique of cooking on a barbecue you can start to become more ambitious. Soon you will progress from burgers for two to meals for large parties of family and friends.

- Make sure the barbecue is sited on a firm surface and is stable and level before lighting. Once the barbecue is lit, do not move it.

- Keep the barbecue sheltered from wind, and keep it well away from trees and shrubs.

- Always follow the manufacturer's instructions for your barbecue, as there are some barbecues that only use one type of fuel.

- Don't try to hasten the fire – some fuels may take quite a time to build up heat. Never pour flammable liquid on to the barbecue.

- Keep children (and pets) away from the fire and always make sure the cooking is supervised by adults.

- Keep perishable foods cold until you're ready to cook – especially in hot weather. If you take them outdoors, place them in a cool bag until needed.

- Make sure meat such as burgers, sausages and poultry are thoroughly cooked – there should be no trace of pink in the juices. Test by piercing the thickest part of the flesh: the juices should run clear and the flesh should not have any trace of pinkness.

- Wash your hands after handling raw meats and before touching other foods; don't use the same utensils for raw ingredients and cooked food.

- It's a good idea to pre-cook poultry in the microwave or oven and then transfer them straight to the barbecue, to finish off. Don't allow the meat to cool down between the microwave or oven and the barbecue. Poultry should not be reheated once it has cooled.

- In case the fire should get out of control have a bucket of sand and a water spray on hand, to douse the flames.

- Keep a first-aid kit handy. If someone burns themselves hold the burn under running water.

- Trim excess fat from meat and don't use too much oil in marinades; fat can cause dangerous flare-ups if too much drips on to the hot fuel.

- Use long-handled barbecue tools, such as forks, tongs and brushes, for turning and basting food; keep some oven gloves handy, preferably the extra-long type to protect your hands.

- Keep raw foods to be cooked away from foods that are ready to eat, to prevent possible cross-contamination.

Barbecue Tools and Equipment

Special barbecue tools are by no means essential, but many of them do make the job easier and often safer. The following are some of the best.

Long-handled barbecue tools
These should include a pair of tongs, a fork and a flat slice for turning and lifting foods. Choose tools with wooden or heatproof handles, so they do not get too hot to hold.

Long-handled basting brushes
These are for basting food and oiling the grill rack. Choose those with real bristles, not nylon, which could melt or burn in use.

Skewers
For kebabs flat metal skewers are good, particularly for meats, as they conduct the heat well; many have long heatproof handles or even hand-shields. Bamboo and wooden ones are inexpensive and disposable. They're good for all types of food, but should be soaked in water before use, to prevent them from burning.

Hinged wire racks
These are useful for cooking and turning delicate items, such as whole fish, to prevent them from breaking up.

Oven gloves
Thick oven gloves, or a cloth will protect your hands from the fire. Choose well-padded cloth gloves.

Apron
An apron will protect you and your clothes from the fire and splashing fat. It should be heavy-duty cotton, rather than plastic-coated.

Meat thermometer
A good thermometer will give a reading of the inside temperature of a large joint of meat. Take care not to touch the bone or the spit when you insert it, or you may get a false reading.

Chopping board
Use a heavy wooden board for cutting up food. Use different boards for meat to avoid cross contamination.

Knife
Use a good sharp knife and again avoid cross contamination by using a different one for meat.

Water spray
Similar to the type used for spraying house plants, a spray is useful for cooling the fire or dousing flames if it gets too hot.

Stiff wire brush
Use this or an abrasive pad and scraper to clean grill racks after cooking. Use with detergent or a special spray-on barbecue cleaner.

oven glove

apron

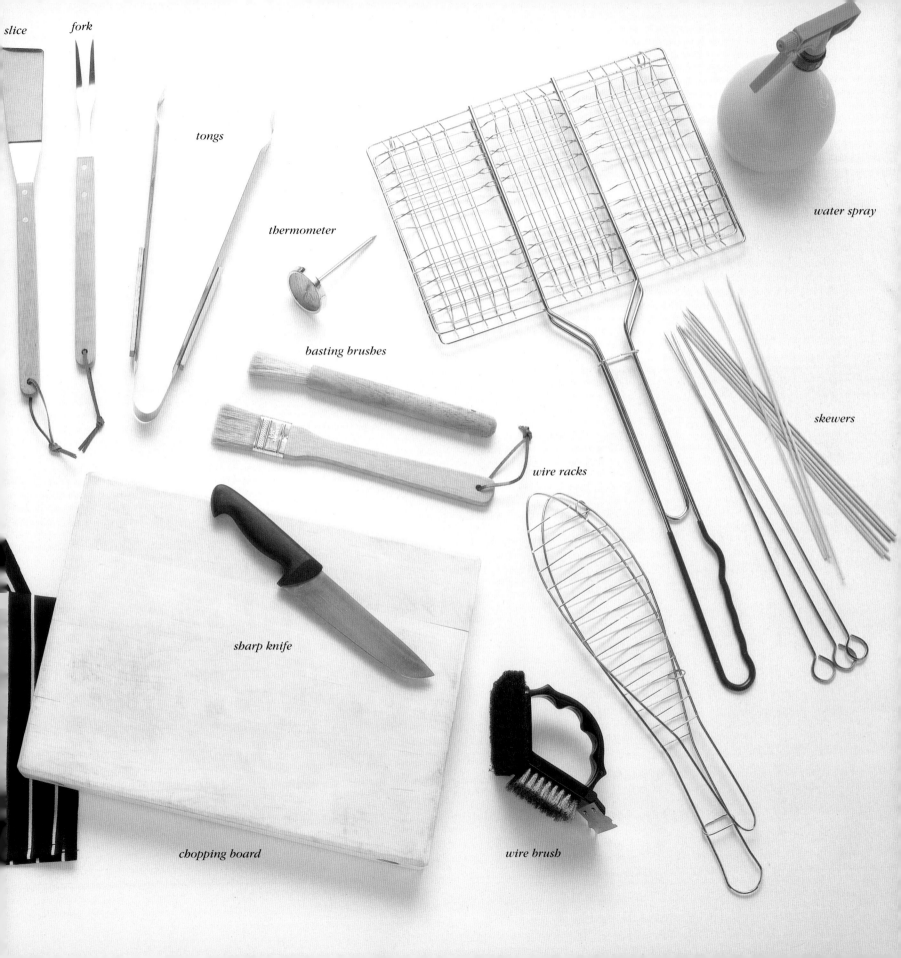

slice

fork

tongs

thermometer

basting brushes

water spray

skewers

wire racks

sharp knife

chopping board

wire brush

Basic Timing Guide for Barbecue Cooking

Giving accurate timings for barbecuing foods is almost impossible, as the heat will vary depending on the type and size of barbecue, the type of fuel used, the height of the grill from the fire and, of course, the weather. Cooking times will also be affected by the thickness and type of food, the quality and tenderness of the meat, and whereabouts on the grill it is actually placed.

Bearing this in mind, you should use the chart below only as a rough guide for timing. Always carefully test the food to make sure it is thoroughly cooked or done to your own taste. You may prefer beef or lamb slightly pink inside, for instance, but chicken or pork should always be cooked until the juices are clear and the flesh shows no trace of pink.
The times in the chart are for

total cooking time, allowing for turning the food as necessary. Most foods need turning only once, but small items, such as kebabs or sausages, may need to be turned more frequently, to ensure even cooking. Foods cooked in foil will take longer to cook.

If your barbecue allows you to adjust the height of the grill rack, this is the easiest way to adjust the heat of the fire

during cooking. For a medium heat, the rack should be about 10 cm/4 in from the fire. Raise or lower this to obtain a lower or higter heat. If you wish to sear food, such as steaks, over a very high heat, move the rack to 4–5 cm/1½–2 in from the fire and then finish cooking on a lower heat. If the barbecue has air vents, you can also use these to control the heat.

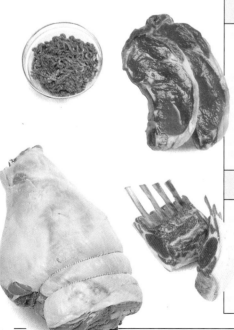

Type of Food	Weight or Thickness	Heat	Cooking Time (total)
Beef			
steaks	2.5 cm/1 in	hot	rare: 5 minutes medium: 8 minutes well done: 12 minutes
burgers	2 cm/³⁄₄ in	hot	6–8 minutes
kebabs	2.5 cm/1 in	hot	5–8 minutes
joints, e.g. rump or sirloin	1.5 kg/3½ lb	spit	2–3 hours
Lamb			
leg steaks	2cm /³⁄₄ in	medium	10–15 minutes
chops	2.5 cm/1 in	medium	10–15 minutes
kebabs	2.5 cm/1 in	medium	6–15 minutes
butterfly leg	8 cm/3 in	low	rare: 40–45 minutes well done: 1 hour
rolled shoulder	1.5 kg/3½ lb	spit	1¼–1½ hours

Type of Food	Weight or Thickness	Heat	Cooking Time (total)
Pork			
chops	2.5 cm/1 in	medium	15–18 minutes
kebabs	2.5 cm/1 in	medium	12–15 minutes
spare ribs		medium	30–40 minutes
sausages	thick	medium	8–10 minutes
joints, e.g.			
shoulder or loin	1.5 kg/3½ lb	spit	2–3 hours
Chicken			
whole	1.5 kg/3½ lb	spit	1–1¼ hours
quarters, leg or			
breast		medium	30–35 minutes
boneless breasts		medium	10–15 minutes
drumsticks		medium	25–30 minutes
kebabs		medium	6–10 minutes
poussin, whole	450 g/1 lb	spit	25–30 minutes
poussin,			
spatchcocked	450 g/1 lb	medium	25–30 minutes
Duckling			
whole	2.25 kg/5 lb	spit	1–1½ hours
half		medium	35–45 minutes
breasts, boneless		medium	15–20 minutes
Fish			
large, whole	2.25–4.5 kg/5–10 lb	low/medium	allow 10 minutes per 2.5 cm/1 in thickness
small, whole	500–900 kg/1¼–2 lb	hot/medium	12–20 minutes
sardines		hot/medium	4–6 minutes
fish steaks			
or fillets	2.5 cm/1 in	medium	6–10 minutes
kebabs	2.5 cm/1 in	medium	5–8 minutes
large prawns,			
in shell		medium	6–8 minutes
large prawns,			
shelled		medium	4–6 minutes
scallops/mussels,			
in shell		medium	until open
scallops/mussels,			
shelled, skewered		medium	5–8 minutes
half lobster		low/medium	15–20 minutes

Lighting the Fire

Follow these basic instructions for lighting the fire, unless you have self-igniting charcoal, in which case you should follow the manufacturer's instructions.

1 Spread a layer of foil over the base of the barbecue, to reflect the heat and make cleaning easier.

2 Spread a layer of wood, charcoal or briquettes on the fire grate about 5 cm/2 in deep. Pile the fuel in a small pyramid in the centre.

3 Push one or two firelighter cubes into the centre of the pyramid or pour about 45 ml/3 tbsp of liquid firelighter into the fuel and leave for 1 minute. Light with a long match or taper and leave to burn for 15 minutes. Spread the coals evenly and then leave for 30–45 minutes, until the coals are covered with a film of grey ash, before cooking.

Controlling the Heat

There are three basic ways to control the heat of the barbecue during cooking.

1 Raise or lower the height of the grill rack. Raise it for slow cooking, or use the bottom level for searing foods.

2 Push the burning coals apart, for a lower heat; pile them closer together, to increase the heat of the fire.

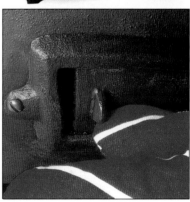

3 Most barbecues have air vents to allow air to the fire. Open them to make the fire hotter, or close them to lower the temperature.

Cooking in Foil Parcels

Delicate foods, or foods that are best cooked slowly in their own steam, can be cooked in foil parcels and either placed directly into the coals of the fire or on the barbecue rack. You can wrap all kinds of flavourings in the foil parcels, too.

Preparing Whole Fish for Grilling

Small whole fish are ideal for barbecuing, especially oily fish such as mackerel or trout. Often they will already be prepared by the fishmonger, but if not they are very simple to do at home.

1 Use heavy-duty cooking foil and cut two equal pieces, to make a double thickness, large enough to wrap the food. Lightly brush the centre of the foil with melted butter or oil.

2 Place the food in the centre of the foil and add any flavourings and seasonings. Pull up the edges of the foil, on opposite sides, over the food.

1 Cut off the fins and strip out the gills with scissors.

2 Hold the fish firmly at the tail end and use the back of a small knife blade or a special scaling gadget to remove the scales, scraping towards the head end. Rinse under cold water.

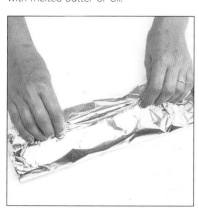

3 Make a double fold in the top of the foil.

4 Fold over the ends, or twist them together, making sure the parcel is sealed completely, so the juices cannot escape during cooking.

3 Cut a long slit under the fish, from just under the tail to just behind the gills, to open up the belly. Use the knife to push out the entrails and discard them. Rinse the fish in cold water.

4 Rub the inside cavity of the fish with salt and rinse again; then dry with absorbent kitchen paper.

A Basic Burger

The simplest of barbecue foods and perhaps the most universally enjoyed, burgers are easy to make and much nicer and more versatile than the ones you can buy.

Makes 4

115 g/4 oz/1 cup minced beef or
   other meat
5 ml/1 tsp mixed dried or
   chopped fresh herbs
salt and freshly ground black
   pepper

1 Place the minced beef or other meat in a bowl and thoroughly break up with a fork.

2 Add the herbs and season well.

3 Bring the mixture together with your hands and form into four burgers. Cook on a moderately-hot barbecue for about 8 minutes, turning once.

VARIATION

For cheeseburgers use the basic burger base, after breaking up the minced beef with a fork, add

15 ml/1 tbsp tomato purée and 30 ml/2 tbsp grated cheese. Mix well then follow steps 2 and 3.

Stilton Burger

A more sophisticated version of the cheeseburger.

Makes 4

450 g/1 lb/4 cups minced beef
1 onion, finely chopped
1 celery stick, finely chopped
5 ml/1 tsp dried mixed herbs
5 ml/1 tsp prepared mustard
50 g/2 oz/½ cup crumbled
   Stilton cheese

1 Place the minced beef in a bowl together with the onion and celery, season well. Stir in the dried herbs and mustard and mix together to form a firm mixture.

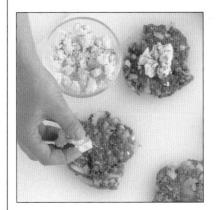

2 Divide the mixture into eight equal portions, place four on a chopping board and flatten slightly. Place the crumbled cheese in the centre of each.

3 Flatten the remaining mixture and place on top. Mould the mixture to encase the crumbled cheese and shape into four burgers. Cook on the barbecue for 12 minutes, turning once.

Relishes

These relishes are very easy and quick to prepare and will liven up sausages, burgers and steaks.

QUICK BARBECUE RELISH

Making use of storecupboard ingredients, this quick relish is ideal for an impromptu barbecue. It has a tangy flavour.

45 ml/3 tbsp sweet pickle
15 ml/1 tbsp Worcestershire
 sauce
30 ml/2 tbsp tomato ketchup
10 ml/2 tsp prepared mustard
15 ml/1 tbsp cider vinegar
30 ml/2 tbsp brown sauce

1 Mix together the pickle, Worcestershire sauce, tomato ketchup and prepared mustard.

2 Add the vinegar and brown sauce and mix well. Cover and chill and use when required.

TOMATO RELISH

A cooked relish which may be served hot or cold with a concentrated tomato flavour. Ideal with barbecued fish and meat.

15 ml/1 tbsp olive oil
1 onion, finely chopped
1 garlic clove, crushed
25 g/1 oz/2 tbsp flour
30 ml/2 tbsp tomato ketchup
300 ml/½ pint/1¼ cups passata
5 ml/1 tsp sugar
15 ml/1 tbsp fresh parsley,
 chopped

1 Heat the oil in a pan. Add the onion and garlic clove and fry for 5 minutes. Add the flour and cook for 1 minute.

2 Stir in the tomato ketchup, passata, sugar and fresh parsley. Bring to the boil and cook for 10 minutes. Cover and chill and use when required.

COOK'S TIP

Barbecue and Tomato relishes should be used as quickly as possible, but will keep for a few days in the fridge.

VARIATION

For a hot and spicy version of this relish, add 10 ml/2 tsp chilli sauce and 1 green chilli, finely chopped at step two.

CUCUMBER RELISH

A cool, refreshing relish, it may also be used as a dip with crudités as a starter.

½ cucumber
2 celery sticks, chopped
1 green pepper, seeded and
 chopped
1 garlic clove, crushed
300 ml/½ pint/1¼ cups natural
 yoghurt
15 ml/1 tbsp chopped fresh
 coriander
freshly ground black pepper

1 Dice the cucumber and place in a large bowl. Add the celery, green pepper and crushed garlic.

2 Stir in the yoghurt and fresh coriander. Season with the pepper. Cover and chill. Use the same day.

Marinating

Marinades are used to add flavour, moisten or tenderize foods, particularly meat. Marinades can be either savoury or sweet and are as varied as you want to make them; spicy, fruity, fragrant or exotic. Certain classic combinations always work well with certain foods. Usually, it's best to choose oily marinades for dry foods, such as lean meat or white fish, and wine- or vinegar-based marinades for rich foods with a higher fat content. Most marinades don't contain salt, which can draw out the juices from meat; it's best to add salt just before cooking.

1 Place the food for marinating in a wide dish or bowl, preferably large enough to allow it to lie in a single layer.

2 Mix together the ingredients for the marinade thoroughly.

3 Pour the marinade over the food and turn the food, to coat it evenly.

4 Cover the dish and refrigerate from 30 minutes up to several hours, depending on the recipe, turning the food over occasionally, and spooning the marinade over it.

5 Remove the food with a slotted spoon, or lift it out with tongs, and drain off and reserve the marinade. If necessary, allow the food to come to room temperature before cooking.

6 Use the marinade for basting or brushing the food, during cooking.

Marinades For Barbecues

BASIC BARBECUE MARINADE

This can be used for meat or fish.

1 garlic clove, crushed
45 ml/3 tbsp sunflower or
   olive oil
45 ml/3 tbsp dry sherry
15 ml/1 tbsp Worcestershire
   sauce
15 ml/1 tbsp dark soy sauce
freshly ground black pepper

HERB MARINADE

This is good for fish, meat or poultry.

120 ml/4 fl oz/½ cup dry white wine
60 ml/4 tbsp olive oil
15 ml/1 tbsp lemon juice
30 ml/2 tbsp finely chopped fresh
   herbs, such as parsley, thyme,
   chives or basil
freshly ground black pepper

COOK'S TIP

The amount of marinade you
will need depends on the
amount of the food but, as a
rough guide, about 150 ml/
¼ pint/⅔ cup is enough for
about 500 g/1¼ lb of food.

HONEY CITRUS MARINADE

This is good with fish or chicken.

finely grated rind and juice of
   ½ lime, ½ lemon and ½ small
   orange
45 ml/3 tbsp sunflower oil
30 ml/2 tbsp clear honey
15 ml/1 tbsp soy sauce
5 ml/1 tsp Dijon mustard
freshly ground black pepper

YOGURT SPICE MARINADE

For fish, meats or poultry.

150 ml/¼ pint/⅔ cup natural
   yogurt
1 small onion, finely chopped
1 garlic clove, crushed
5 ml/1 tsp finely chopped fresh
   root ginger
5 ml/1 tsp ground coriander
5 ml/1 tsp ground cumin
2.5 ml/½ tsp ground turmeric

RED WINE MARINADE

Good with red meats and game.

150 ml/¼ pint/⅔ cup dry red
   wine
15 ml/1 tbsp olive oil
15 ml/1 tbsp red-wine vinegar
2 garlic cloves, crushed
2 dried bay leaves, crumbled
freshly ground black pepper

Minty Lamb Burgers with Redcurrant Chutney

These rather special burgers take a little extra time to prepare, but are well worth it.

Serves 4

500 g/1¼ lb minced lean lamb
1 small onion, finely chopped
30 ml/2 tbsp finely chopped
    fresh mint
30 ml/2 tbsp finely chopped
    fresh parsley
115 g/4 oz mozzarella cheese
salt and freshly ground black
    pepper

FOR THE CHUTNEY
115 g/4 oz/1½ cups fresh or
    frozen redcurrants
10 ml/2 tsp clear honey
5 ml/1 tsp balsamic vinegar
30 ml/2 tbsp finely chopped
    mint

redcurrants

mint

minced lamb

balsamic vinegar

clear honey

mozzarella cheese   *parsley*

onion

COOK'S TIP

If time is short, or if fresh redcurrants are not available, serve the burgers with redcurrant sauce from a jar.

1 Mix together the lamb, onion, mint and parsley until evenly combined; season well with salt and pepper.

2 Divide the mixture into eight equal pieces and use your hands to press them into flat rounds.

3 Cut the mozzarella into four slices or cubes. Place them on four of the lamb rounds. Top each with another round of meat mixture.

4 Press together firmly, making four flattish burger shapes and sealing in the cheese completely.

5 Place all the ingredients for the chutney in a bowl and mash them together with a fork. Season well with salt and pepper.

6 Brush the lamb patties with oil and cook them over a moderately hot barbecue for about 15 minutes, turning once, until golden brown. Serve with the redcurrant chutney.

Bacon Kofta Kebabs and Salad

Kofta kebabs can be made with any type of minced meat, but bacon is very successful if you have a food processor.

Serves 4

250 g/9 oz lean streaky bacon
   rashers, chopped
1 small onion, chopped
1 celery stick, chopped
75 ml/5 tbsp fresh wholemeal
   breadcrumbs
45 ml/3 tbsp chopped fresh
   thyme
30 ml/2 tbsp Worcestershire
   sauce
1 egg, beaten
salt and freshly ground black
   pepper
oil for brushing

For the salad
115 g/4 oz/³⁄₄ cup bulgur wheat
60 ml/4 tbsp toasted sunflower
   seeds
15 ml/1 tbsp olive oil
handful celery leaves, chopped

streaky bacon rashers

onion

bulgur wheat   *sunflower seeds*

wholemeal breadcrumbs

olive oil

celery   *Worcestershire sauce*   *egg*

1 Place the bacon, onion, celery and breadcrumbs in a food processor and process until finely chopped. Add the thyme, Worcestershire sauce, salt, pepper and enough beaten egg to bind to a firm mixture.

2 Divide the mixture into eight even pieces and use your hands to shape the pieces around eight bamboo skewers.

3 For the grain salad, place the bulgur wheat in a large bowl and pour over boiling water to cover. Leave to stand for 30 minutes, until the grains are tender.

4 Drain well and stir in the sunflower seeds, oil, salt and pepper. Stir in the celery leaves.

5 Cook the kofta skewers over a medium-hot barbecue for 8–10 minutes, turning occasionally, until golden brown. Serve with the salad.

Tex-Mex Burgers in Tortillas

If you fancy a change from ordinary burgers in baps, try this easy Tex-Mex version. Serve with a crisp green salad.

Serves 4

500 g/1¼ lb lean minced beef
1 small onion, finely chopped
1 small green pepper, seeded
   and finely chopped
1 garlic clove, crushed
oil for brushing
4 fresh tortillas
chopped fresh coriander, to
   garnish

FOR THE GUACAMOLE SAUCE
2 ripe avocados
1 garlic clove, crushed
2 tomatoes, chopped
juice of 1 lime or lemon
½ small green chilli, chopped
30 ml/2 tbsp chopped fresh
   coriander
salt and freshly ground black
   pepper

minced beef

green pepper

green chilli

lime   *coriander*

onion

garlic   *avocados*

oil

COOK'S TIP

The guacamole sauce should be made not more than about an hour before it's needed, or it will start to brown. If it has to be left to stand, sprinkle a little extra lime juice over the top and stir it in just before serving.

1 Mix together the minced beef, onion, pepper and garlic, and then season well with salt and pepper.

2 Using your hands, shape the mixture into four large, round burgers and brush them with oil.

3 For the guacamole sauce, cut the avocados in half, remove the stone and scoop out the flesh.

4 Mash the avocado flesh roughly and mix in the garlic, tomatoes, lime juice, chilli and coriander. Adjust the seasoning with salt and pepper.

5 Cook the burgers on a medium hot barbecue for 8–10 minutes, turning once, until golden brown.

6 When the burgers are almost cooked, heat the tortillas quickly on the barbecue for about 15 seconds each side and then place a spoonful of guacamole and a burger on each. Wrap the tortilla round the filling to serve, garnished with coriander.

Barbecued Lamb with Potato Slices

A traditional mixture of fresh herbs adds a really summery flavour in this simple lamb dish. A leg of lamb is easier to cook evenly on the barbecue if it's boned out, or "butterflied" first, and it's so much easier to carve!

COOK'S TIP
If you have a spit-roasting attachment, the lamb can be rolled and tied with herbs inside and spit roasted for 1–1½ hours. You can cook larger pieces of lamb on the spit.

Serves 4

1 leg of lamb, about 1.75 kg/ 4½ lb
1 garlic clove, sliced thinly
handful of fresh flat-leaved parsley
handful of fresh sage
handful of fresh rosemary
handful of fresh thyme
90 ml/6 tbsp dry sherry
60 ml/4 tbsp walnut oil
500 g/1¼ lb medium-size potatoes
salt and freshly ground black pepper

dry sherry

walnut oil

leg of lamb

potatoes

garlic

sage *rosemary*

flat-leaved parsley *thyme*

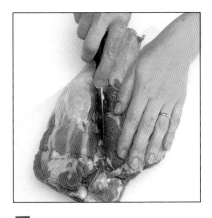

1 Place the lamb on a board, smooth side downwards, so that you can see where the bone lies. Using a sharp knife, make a long cut through the flesh down to the bone.

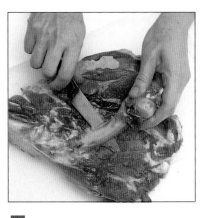

2 Scrape away the meat from the bone on both sides, until the bone is completely exposed. Remove the bone and cut away any sinews and excess fat.

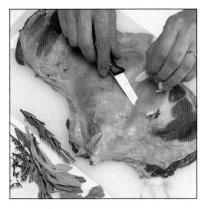

3 Cut through the thickest part of the meat to enable it to open out as flat as possible. Make several cuts in the lamb, with a sharp knife, and push slivers of garlic and sprigs of herbs into them.

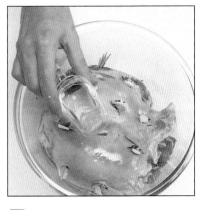

4 Place the meat in a bowl and pour over the sherry and oil. Chop about half the remaining herbs and scatter over the meat. Cover and leave to marinate in the refrigerator for at least 30 minutes.

5 Remove the lamb from the marinade and season, place on a medium-hot barbecue and cook for 30–35 minutes, turning occasionally and basting with the reserved marinade.

6 Scrub the potatoes, then cut them in thick slices. Brush them with the marinade and place them around the lamb. Cook for about 15–20 minutes, turning occasionally, until they are golden brown.

Char-grilled Sausages with Prunes and Bacon

Sausages are a constant barbecue favourite and this is one way to ring the changes. Serve with French bread.

Serves 4

8 large, meaty sausages, such as Toulouse or good-quality pork sausages
30 ml/2 tbsp Dijon mustard
24 ready-to-eat prunes
8 smoked streaky bacon rashers

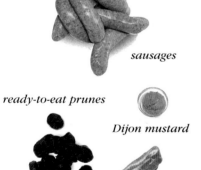

sausages

ready-to-eat prunes

Dijon mustard

smoked streaky bacon rashers

COOK'S TIP

To make sure the bacon stays in place, secure it with cocktail sticks. Soak the sticks in water (to prevent them burning) while the sausages cook; remove the sticks before serving.

1 With a sharp knife, cut a long slit through one side of each sausage, cutting them about three-quarters of the way through.

2 Spread the cut surface with mustard and then place three prunes in each sausage, pressing them in firmly.

3 Stretch the bacon rashers out thinly with the back of a knife.

4 Wrap the bacon round the sausages, to hold them in shape. Cook over a hot barbecue for 15–18 minutes, turning occasionally, until evenly browned and thoroughly cooked.

Five-spice Rib-stickers

Choose the meatiest spare ribs you can find, to make these a real success.

Serves 4

1 kg/2 lb Chinese-style pork
   spare ribs
10 ml/2 tsp Chinese five-spice
   powder
2 garlic cloves, crushed
15 ml/1 tbsp grated fresh root
   ginger
2.5 ml/½ tsp chilli sauce
60 ml/4 tbsp soy sauce
45 ml/3 tbsp dark muscovado
   sugar
15 ml/1 tbsp sunflower oil
4 spring onions

spare ribs

chilli sauce

spring onions

fresh root ginger

dark muscovado sugar

soy sauce

garlic

sunflower oil

Chinese five-spice powder

COOK'S TIP
Make sure you buy the traditional Chinese five-spice powder, not Chinese five-spice seasoning, which is much saltier.

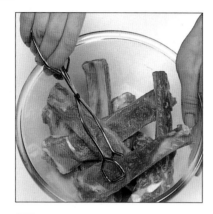

1 If the spare ribs are still attached together, cut between them to separate them (or ask your butcher to do this). Place the spare ribs in a large bowl.

2 Mix together all the remaining ingredients, except the spring onions, and pour over the ribs. Toss well to coat evenly. Cover the bowl and leave to marinate in the refrigerator overnight.

3 Cook the ribs on a medium-hot barbecue, turning frequently, for 30–40 minutes. Brush occasionally with the remaining marinade.

4 Finely slice the spring onions and scatter them over the ribs, to serve.

Ham Pizzettes with Melted Brie and Mango

These little individual pizzas are topped with an unusual combination of smoked ham, Brie and juicy chunks of mango.

Serves 6

225 g/8 oz/2 cups strong white flour
7 g/¼ oz sachet easy-blend dried yeast
150 ml/¼ pint/⅔ cup warm water
60 ml/4 tbsp olive oil

FOR THE TOPPING
1 medium-size ripe mango
150 g/5 oz smoked ham, sliced wafer-thin
150 g/5 oz Brie cheese, diced
12 yellow cherry tomatoes, halved
salt and freshly ground black pepper

smoked ham

strong white flour

mango

Brie cheese

yellow cherry tomatoes

easy-blend yeast   olive oil

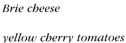

COOK'S TIP

It's important to flatten the dough rounds out quite thinly, and to cook them fairly slowly, or the pizzettes will not cook evenly. To save time, you can use a 300 g/11 oz packet of pizza dough mix.

1 In a large bowl, stir together the flour and yeast, with a pinch of salt. Make a well in the centre and stir in the water and 45 ml/3 tbsp of the oil. Stir until thoroughly mixed.

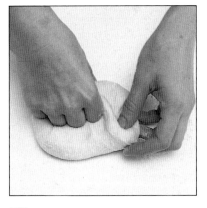

2 Turn the dough out on to a floured surface and knead it for about 5 minutes, or until it's smooth.

3 Return the dough to the bowl and cover it with a damp cloth or oiled clear film. Leave in a warm place for about 30 minutes or until the dough is doubled in size and springy to the touch.

4 Divide the dough into six and roll each piece into a ball. Flatten out with your hand and use your knuckles to press each piece of dough to a round of about 15 cm/6 in diameter, with a raised lip around the edge.

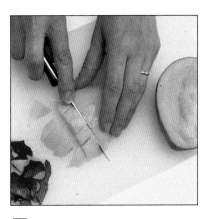

5 Halve, stone and peel the mango and cut it into small dice. Arrange with the ham on top of each piece of dough. Top with cheese and tomatoes and sprinkle with salt and pepper.

6 Drizzle the remaining oil over the pizzettes, then place them on a medium-hot barbecue and cook for 8–10 minutes, until they are golden brown and crisp underneath.

Pork and Pineapple Satay

This variation on the classic satay has added pineapple, but keeps the traditional coconut and peanut sauce.

Serves 4

500 g/1¼ lb pork fillet
1 small onion, chopped
1 garlic clove, chopped
60 ml/4 tbsp soy sauce
finely grated rind of ½ lemon
5 ml/1 tsp ground cumin
5 ml/1 tsp ground coriander
5 ml/1 tsp ground turmeric
5 ml/1 tsp dark muscovado sugar
225 g/8 oz can pineapple chunks, or 1 small fresh pineapple, peeled and diced
salt and freshly ground black pepper

FOR THE SATAY SAUCE
175 ml/6 fl oz/³⁄₄ cup coconut milk
115 g/4 oz/6 tbsp crunchy peanut butter
1 garlic clove, crushed
10 ml/2 tsp soy sauce
5 ml/1 tsp dark muscovado sugar

coconut milk

pineapple chunks

pork fillet

crunchy peanut butter

soy sauce

dark muscovado sugar

onion   garlic

ground coriander

ground cumin   chilli powder

ground turmeric

1 Trim any fat from the pork fillet and cut it in 2.5 cm/1 in cubes. Place the meat in a large bowl.

2 Place the onion, garlic, soy sauce, lemon rind, spices and sugar in a blender or food processor. Add two pieces of pineapple and process until the mixture is almost smooth.

4 For the sauce, pour the coconut milk into a small pan and stir in the peanut butter. Stir in the remaining sauce ingredients and heat gently over the barbecue, stirring until smooth and hot. Cover and keep warm on the edge of the barbecue.

COOK'S TIP

If you cannot buy coconut milk, look out for creamed coconut in a block. Dissolve a 50 g/2 oz piece in 150 ml/¼ pint/²⁄₃ cup boiling water and use as below.

3 Add the paste to the pork, tossing well to coat evenly. Thread the pieces of pork on to bamboo skewers, with the remaining pineapple.

5 Cook the pork and pineapple skewers on a medium-hot barbecue for 10–12 minutes, turning occasionally, until golden brown and thoroughly cooked. Serve with the satay sauce.

Mixed Grill Skewers with Horseradish Butter

A hearty, classic selection of meats all cooked together on a skewer, drizzled with a delicious hot horseradish butter. Vary the meats as you like, but keep them all about the same thickness so they cook evenly.

Serves 4

4 small lamb noisettes, about
   2.5 cm/1 in thick
4 lamb's kidneys
4 streaky bacon rashers
8 cherry tomatoes
8 chipolata sausages
12–16 bay leaves

FOR THE HORSERADISH BUTTER:
30 ml/2 tbsp horseradish relish
45 ml/3 tbsp melted butter
salt and freshly ground black
   pepper

streaky bacon rashers

chipolata sausages

lamb's kidneys

lamb noisettes

melted butter

horseradish sauce

bay leaves

cherry tomatoes

COOK'S TIP
Try using your favourite mustard instead of horseradish, for a tangy mustard butter.

1 Trim any excess fat from the lamb noisettes. Halve the kidneys and remove the cores with scissors.

2 Cut each rasher of bacon in half across the middle and wrap each piece around a tomato or a half-kidney.

3 Thread the lamb, kidneys, tomatoes, chipolatas and bay leaves on to four long metal skewers.

4 Stir together the horseradish and butter until thoroughly mixed.

5 Brush a little of the horseradish butter over the meat and sprinkle with salt and pepper.

6 Cook on a medium-hot barbecue for 12–15 minutes, turning occasionally, until golden brown and thoroughly cooked. Serve with the remaining horseradish butter poured over.

Racks of Lamb with Lavender Balsamic Marinade

Lavender is an unusual flavour to use with meat, but its heady, summery scent really works well with grilled lamb. If you prefer, rosemary can take its place.

Serves 4

4 racks of lamb, with 3–4 cutlets
  each
1 shallot, finely chopped
45 ml/3 tbsp chopped fresh
  lavender
15 ml/1 tbsp balsamic vinegar
30 ml/2 tbsp olive oil
15 ml/1 tbsp lemon juice
salt and freshly ground black
  pepper
handful of lavender sprigs

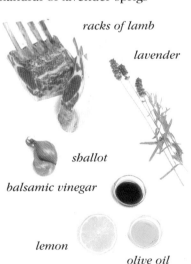

racks of lamb

lavender

shallot

balsamic vinegar

lemon

olive oil

COOK'S TIP

Instead of rack of lamb, individual cutlets can be cooked in this way; allow 10–15 minutes, turning occasionally.

1 Place the racks of lamb in a large bowl or wide dish and sprinkle over the chopped shallot.

2 Sprinkle the lavender over the lamb.

3 Beat together the vinegar, oil and lemon juice and pour them over the lamb. Season well with salt and pepper and then turn to coat evenly.

4 Scatter a few lavender sprigs over the grill or on the coals of a medium-hot barbecue. Cook the lamb for 15–20 minutes, turning once and basting with any remaining marinade, until golden brown and still slightly pink in the centre.

Peppered Steaks in Beer and Garlic

Robust flavours for hearty appetites. Serve with salad and jacket potatoes.

Serves 4

4 beef sirloin or rump steaks, 2.5 cm/1 in thick, about 175 g/ 6 oz each
2 garlic cloves, crushed
120 ml/4 fl oz/½ cup brown ale or stout
30 ml/2 tbsp dark muscovado sugar
30 ml/2 tbsp Worcestershire sauce
15 ml/1 tbsp corn oil
15 ml/1 tbsp crushed black peppercorns

dark muscovado sugar

brown ale

beef steaks

Worcestershire sauce

garlic

corn oil

black peppercorns

COOK'S TIP
Take care when basting with the reserved marinade, as the alcohol will tend to flare up; spoon or brush on just a small amount at a time.

I Place the steaks in a deep dish and add the garlic, ale or stout, sugar, Worcestershire sauce and oil. Turn to coat evenly in the marinade, and then leave to marinate in the refrigerator for 2–3 hours or overnight.

2 Remove the steaks from the dish and reserve the marinade. Sprinkle the peppercorns over the steaks and press them into the surface.

3 Cook the steaks on a hot barbecue, basting them occasionally during cooking, with the reserved marinade.

4 Turn the steaks once during cooking, and cook them for 3–6 minutes on each side, depending on how rare you like them.

Blackened Cajun Chicken and Corn

This is a classic Deep-South method of cooking in a spiced coating, which can be used for poultry, meat or fish. Traditionally, the spiced coating should begin to char and blacken slightly at the edges.

Serves 4

8 chicken joints, eg drumsticks, thighs or wings
2 whole corn cobs
10 ml/2 tsp garlic salt
10 ml/2 tsp ground black pepper
7.5 ml/1½ tsp ground cumin
7.5 ml/1½ tsp paprika
5 ml/1 tsp cayenne pepper
45 ml/3 tbsp melted butter
chopped parsley, to garnish

corn cobs

chicken joints

ground black pepper

melted butter

garlic salt

paprika   *cayenne pepper*

ground cumin

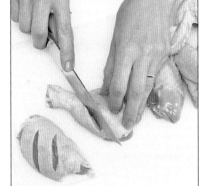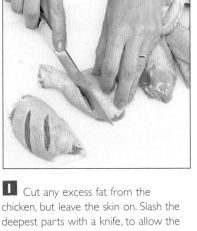

1 Cut any excess fat from the chicken, but leave the skin on. Slash the deepest parts with a knife, to allow the flavours to penetrate.

2 Pull the husks and silks off the corn cobs and cut them into thick slices.

3 Mix together all the spices. Brush the chicken and corn with melted butter and sprinkle the spices over them. Toss well to coat evenly.

4 Cook the chicken pieces on a medium-hot barbecue for about 25 minutes, turning occasionally. Add the corn after 15 minutes, and grill, turning often, until golden brown. Serve garnished with chopped parsley.

Turkey Rolls with Gazpacho Sauce

This Spanish-style recipe uses quick-cooking turkey steaks, but you could also cook veal escalopes in the same way.

Serves 4

FOR THE SAUCE
1 green pepper, seeded and chopped
1 red pepper, seeded and chopped
7.5 cm/3 in piece cucumber
1 medium-size tomato
1 garlic clove
45 ml/3 tbsp olive oil
15 ml/1 tbsp red wine vinegar

FOR THE TURKEY ROLLS
4 turkey breast steaks
15 ml/1 tbsp red pesto or tomato purée
4 chorizo sausages
salt and freshly ground black pepper

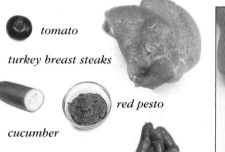
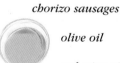

tomato
turkey breast steaks
red pesto
cucumber
chorizo sausages
olive oil
red wine vinegar
red pepper
garlic clove   *green pepper*

1 To make the gazpacho sauce, place the peppers, cucumber, tomato, garlic, 30 ml/2 tbsp of the oil and the vinegar in a food processor and process until almost smooth. Season to taste with salt and pepper and set aside.

2 If the turkey breast steaks are quite thick, place them between two sheets of clear film and beat them with the side of a rolling pin, to flatten them slightly.

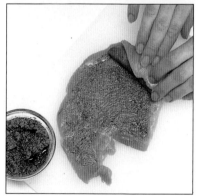

3 Spread the pesto or tomato purée over the turkey and then place a chorizo on each piece and roll up firmly.

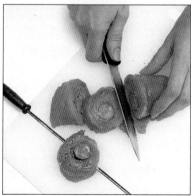

4 Slice the rolls thickly and thread them on to skewers. Grill on a medium-hot barbecue for 10–12 minutes, turning once; serve with the gazpacho sauce.

Chicken Wings Teriyaki-style

This simple, oriental glaze can be used with any cut of chicken or with fish.

Serves 4

1 garlic clove, crushed
45 ml/3 tbsp soy sauce
30 ml/2 tbsp dry sherry
10 ml/2 tsp clear honey
10 ml/2 tsp grated fresh root ginger
5 ml/1 tsp sesame oil
12 chicken wings
15 ml/1 tbsp sesame seeds, toasted

sesame seeds

dry sherry

clear honey

chicken wings

fresh root ginger

garlic

COOK'S TIP

Toasting the sesame seeds lightly helps to bring out their flavour: to do this, either put them in a heavy pan over a moderate heat and stir until golden, or sprinkle on a baking sheet and cook under a medium grill, until golden.

1 Place the garlic, soy sauce, sherry, honey, ginger and sesame oil in a large bowl and beat with a fork, to mix evenly.

2 Add the chicken wings and toss thoroughly, to coat in the marinade. Cover and leave in the refrigerator for about 30 minutes or longer.

3 Cook the wings on a fairly hot barbecue for 20–25 minutes, turning occasionally and brushing with the remaining marinade.

4 Sprinkle with sesame seeds and serve with a crisp green salad.

Chicken with Herb and Ricotta Stuffing

These little chicken drumsticks are full of flavour and the stuffing and bacon helps to keep them moist and tender.

Serves 4

60 ml/4 tbsp ricotta cheese
1 garlic clove, crushed
45 ml/3 tbsp mixed chopped fresh herbs, eg chives, flat-leaved parsley and mint
30 ml/2 tbsp fresh brown breadcrumbs
8 chicken drumsticks
8 rashers smoked streaky bacon
5 ml/1 tsp whole-grain mustard
15 ml/1 tbsp sunflower oil
salt and freshly ground black pepper

fresh brown breadcrumbs

chicken drumsticks

ricotta cheese

sunflower oil

whole-grain mustard

smoked streaky bacon rashers

chives

garlic *flat-leaved parsley*

1 Mix together the ricotta, garlic, herbs and breadcrumbs. Season well with salt and pepper.

2 Carefully loosen the skin from each drumstick and spoon a little of the herb stuffing under each, smoothing the skin back over firmly.

3 Wrap a bacon rasher around the wide end of each drumstick, to hold the skin in place over the stuffing

4 Mix together the mustard and oil and brush them over the chicken. Cook on a medium-hot barbecue for about 25 minutes, turning occasionally, until the juices run clear and not pink when the flesh is pierced.

Baby Chickens with Lime and Chilli

Poussins are small birds which are ideal for one to two portions. The best way to cook them is spatchcocked – flattened out – to ensure more even cooking.

Serves 4

4 poussins or Cornish hens,
  about 450 g/1 lb each
45 ml/3 tbsp butter
30 ml/2 tbsp sun-dried tomato
  paste
finely grated rind of 1 lime
10 ml/2 tsp chilli sauce
juice of ¹/₂ lime
flat-leaved parsley sprigs, to
  garnish
lime wedges, to serve

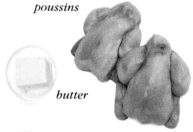

poussins

butter

sun-dried tomato paste

lime   *chilli sauce*

COOK'S TIP

If you wish to serve half a poussin per portion, you may find it easier simply to cut the birds in half lengthways. Use poultry shears or a large sharp knife to cut through the breastbone and backbone.

1 Place each poussin on a board, breast-side upwards, and press down firmly with your hand, to break the breastbone.

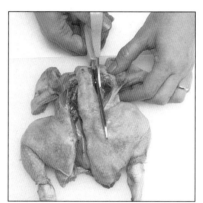

2 Turn the poussin over and, with poultry shears or strong kitchen scissors, cut down either side of the backbone and remove it.

3 Turn the poussin breast-side up and flatten it neatly. Lift the breast skin carefully and gently ease your fingertips underneath, to loosen it from the flesh.

4 Mix together the butter, tomato paste, lime rind and chilli sauce. Spread about three-quarters of the mixture under the skin of each poussin, smoothing it evenly.

5 To hold the poussins flat during cooking, thread two skewers through each bird, crossing at the centre. Each skewer should pass through a wing and then out through a drumstick on the other side.

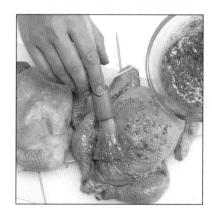

6 Mix the reserved paste with the lime juice and brush it over the skin of the poussins. Cook on a medium-hot barbecue, turning occasionally, for 25–30 minutes, or until there is no trace of pink in the juices when pierced. Garnish with lime wedges and flat-leaved parsley.

Apricot Duck Breasts with Bean Sprout Salad

Duck is rich in fat, so it stays beautifully moist when cooked on a barbecue but any excess fat drains away.

Serves 4

4 plump duck breasts, with skin
1 small red onion, thinly sliced
115 g/4 oz/³/₄ cup ready-to-eat
   dried apricots
15 ml/1 tbsp clear honey
5 ml/1 tsp sesame oil
10 ml/2 tsp ground star anise
salt and freshly ground black
   pepper

FOR THE SALAD
¹/₂ head Chinese leaves, finely
   shredded
150 g/5 oz/2 cups bean sprouts
2 spring onions, shredded
15 ml/1 tbsp light soy sauce
15 ml/1 tbsp groundnut oil
5 ml/1 tsp sesame oil
5 ml/1 tsp clear honey

ready-to-eat dried apricots

duck breasts

spring onions

red onion

sesame oil

Chinese leaves

ground star anise

bean sprouts

clear honey

light soy sauce

1 Place the duck breasts, skin-side down, on a board and cut a long slit down one side, cutting not quite through, to form a large pocket.

2 Tuck the slices of onion and the apricots inside the pocket and press the breast firmly back into shape. Secure with metal skewers.

3 Mix together the honey and sesame oil and brush over the duck, particularly the skin. Sprinkle over the star anise and season with salt and pepper.

4 To make the salad, mix together the shredded Chinese leaves, bean sprouts and spring onions.

COOK'S TIP

If you prefer not to eat the bean sprouts raw, they can be blanched first, by plunging them into boiling water for 1 minute. Drain and rinse in cold water.

5 Shake together all the remaining salad ingredients in a screw-topped jar. Season to taste with salt and pepper. Toss into the salad.

6 Cook the duck over a medium-hot barbecue for 12–15 minutes, turning once, until golden brown. The duck should be slightly pink in the centre.

Chicken Breasts Cooked in Spices and Coconut

This chicken dish can be prepared in advance. Serve it with nan bread.

Serves 4

200 g/7 oz block creamed coconut
300 ml/¹/₂ pint/1¹/₄ cups boiling water
3 garlic cloves, chopped
2 spring onions, chopped
1 fresh green chilli, chopped
5 cm/2 in piece fresh root ginger, chopped
5 ml/1 tsp fennel seeds
2.5 ml/¹/₂ tsp black peppercorns
seeds from 4 cardamom pods
30 ml/2 tbsp ground coriander
5 ml/1 tsp ground cumin
5 ml/1 tsp ground star anise
5 ml/1 tsp ground nutmeg
2.5 ml/¹/₂ tsp ground cloves
2.5 ml/¹/₂ tsp ground turmeric
4 large skinless, boneless chicken breasts
onion rings and fresh coriander sprigs, to garnish

1 Break up the coconut and put it in a jug. Pour the boiling water over and leave to dissolve. Place the garlic, spring onions, chilli, ginger and all the spices in a blender or food processor. Add the coconut mixture and process to a smooth paste.

fresh root ginger

chicken breasts

green chilli

fennel seeds   *spring onions*

nutmegs

garlic

cardamom pods   *creamed coconut*   *black peppercorns*

ground cumin   *ground star anise*

ground coriander   *ground turmeric*   *ground cloves*

2 Make several diagonal cuts across the chicken breasts. Arrange them in one layer in a shallow dish. Spoon over half the coconut mixture and toss well to coat the chicken breasts evenly. Cover the dish and leave to marinate in the fridge for about 30 minutes, or overnight.

3 Cook the chicken on a moderately hot barbecue for 12–15 minutes, turning once, until well browned and thoroughly cooked. Heat the remaining coconut mixture gently, until it's boiling. Serve with the chicken, garnished with onion rings and sprigs of coriander.

Juniper-spiced Venison Chops

Depending on the type of venison available, the chops will vary in size, so you will need either one or two per serving.

Serves 4

4-8 venison chops
250 ml/8 fl oz/1 cup red wine
2 medium-size red onions
6 juniper berries, crushed
1 cinnamon stick, crumbled
1 dried bay leaf, crumbled
thinly pared strip of orange rind
olive oil for brushing
salt and freshly ground black
 pepper

red wine   *venison chops*

bay leaf

red onions

cinnamon stick

olive oil

juniper berries

orange rind

1 Place the venison chops in a large bowl and pour over the wine. Cut the onions in half crossways and add them to the bowl.

2 Add the juniper berries, cinnamon, bay leaf and orange rind. Toss well to coat evenly and then cover the bowl and leave to marinate for about an hour, or overnight.

3 Drain the venison and onions reserving the marinade, brush them with oil and sprinkle with salt and pepper.

4 Cook on a medium-hot barbecue for about 8–10 minutes on each side, turning once and basting with the marinade. The venison should still be slightly pink inside.

Pheasants with Sage and Lemon

Pheasant is quick to cook and makes a really special summer meal. This recipe can also be used for guinea fowl.

Serves 4

2 pheasants, about 450 g/1 lb each
1 lemon
60 ml/4 tbsp chopped fresh sage leaves
3 shallots
5 ml/1 tsp Dijon mustard
15 ml/1 tbsp brandy or dry sherry
150 ml/5 fl oz/²/₃ cup crème fraîche
salt and freshly ground black pepper
lemon wedges and sage sprigs, to garnish

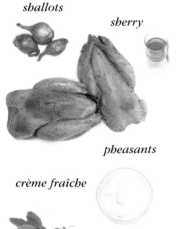

shallots

sherry

pheasants

crème fraîche

sage

Dijon mustard

lemon

COOK'S TIP

Try to choose pheasants which have undamaged skins so that the flavourings stay in place during cooking.

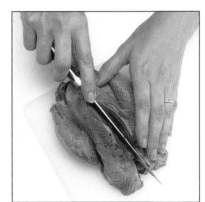

1 Place the pheasants, breast-side upwards, on a board and cut them in half lengthways, using poultry shears or a sharp knife.

2 Finely grate the rind from half the lemon and slice the rest thinly. Mix together the lemon rind and half the chopped sage.

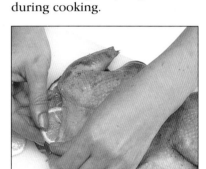

3 Loosen the skin on the breast and legs of the pheasants and push a little of the sage mixture under each. Tuck the lemon slices under the skin, smoothing the skin back firmly.

4 Place each half-pheasant on a medium-hot barbecue grill and cook for 25–30 minutes, turning once.

5 Meanwhile, place the shallots on the barbecue and cook for about 10–12 minutes, turning occasionally, until the skin is blackened and the inside very soft. Peel off the skins, chop the flesh roughly and mash it with the mustard and brandy or sherry.

6 Stir in the crème fraîche and add the reserved chopped sage. Season with salt and pepper. Serve with the pheasants garnished with lemon wedges and sprigs of sage.

Mackerel Kebabs with Sweet Pepper Salad

Mackerel is good for grilling, because its natural oils keep it moist and tasty.

Serves 4

4 medium mackerel, about
  225 g/8 oz each, filleted
2 small red onions, cut in
  wedges
30 ml/2 tbsp chopped fresh
  marjoram
60 ml/4 tbsp dry white wine
45 ml/3 tbsp olive oil
juice of 1 lime

FOR THE SALAD
1 red pepper
1 yellow pepper
1 small red onion
2 large plum tomatoes
15 ml/1 tbsp chopped fresh
  marjoram
10 ml/2 tsp balsamic vinegar
salt and freshly ground black
  pepper

yellow pepper

white wine

red pepper

olive oil

balsamic vinegar

marjoram

mackerel

plum tomatoes

red onions

lime

COOK'S TIP
Other oily fish can be used for this dish: try fillets or cubes of herring, rainbow trout or salmon, instead.

1 Thread each fish fillet on to a skewer, with an onion wedge on each end. Arrange in a shallow dish.

2 Mix together the marjoram, wine, oil and lime juice and spoon over the mackerel. Cover and chill for at least 30 minutes turning once.

3 To make the salad, quarter and seed the peppers and halve the onion. Place the peppers and onions, skin-side down, with the whole tomatoes, on a hot barbecue and leave until the skins are blackened and charred.

4 Remove the vegetables from the barbecue and leave until they are cool enough to handle, then peel off and discard the skins.

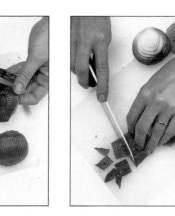

5 Chop the vegetables roughly and put them in a bowl. Stir in the marjoram and balsamic vinegar and season to taste. Toss thoroughly.

6 Remove the kebabs from the fridge and cook on a hot barbecue for 10–12 minutes, occasionally turning and basting them with the marinade. Serve with the pepper salad.

Tiger Prawn Skewers with Walnut Pesto

An unusual starter or main course, which can be prepared in advance and kept in the fridge until you're ready to cook it.

Serves 4

12–16 large, raw shell-on tiger prawns
50 g/2 oz/½ cup walnut pieces
60 ml/4 tbsp chopped fresh flat-leaved parsley
60 ml/4 tbsp chopped fresh basil
2 garlic cloves, chopped
45 ml/3 tbsp grated fresh Parmesan cheese
30 ml/2 tbsp extra virgin olive oil
30 ml/2 tbsp walnut oil
salt and freshly ground black pepper

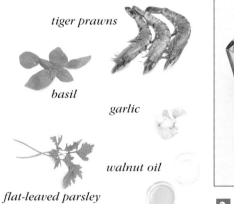

tiger prawns

basil

garlic

walnut oil

flat-leaved parsley

extra-virgin olive oil

Parmesan cheese

walnut pieces

1 Peel the prawns, removing the head but leaving on the tail section. De-vein and then put the prawns in a large bowl.

2 To make the pesto, place the walnuts, parsley, basil, garlic, Parmesan and oils in a blender or food processor and process until very finely chopped. Season with salt and pepper.

3 Add half the pesto to the prawns, toss them well and then cover and chill for a minimum of an hour; or leave them overnight.

4 Thread the prawns on to skewers and cook them on a hot barbecue for 3–4 minutes, turning once. Serve with the remaining pesto and a green salad.

Calamari with Two-Tomato Stuffing

Calamari, or baby squid, are quick to cook, but do turn and baste them often and don't overcook them.

Serves 4

500 g/1¼ lb baby squid, cleaned
1 garlic clove, crushed
3 plum tomatoes, skinned and
    chopped
8 sun-dried tomatoes in oil,
    drained and chopped
60 ml/4 tbsp chopped fresh
    basil, plus extra, to serve
60 ml/4 tbsp fresh white
    breadcrumbs
45 ml/3 tbsp olive oil
15 ml/1 tbsp red wine vinegar
salt and freshly ground black
    pepper
lemon juice, to serve

baby squid

garlic

breadcrumbs

plum tomatoes

sun-dried tomatoes in oil

basil

olive oil

red wine vinegar

1 Remove the tentacles from the squid and roughly chop them; leave the main part of the squid whole.

2 Mix together the garlic, plum tomatoes, sun-dried tomatoes, basil and breadcrumbs. Stir in 15 ml/1 tbsp of the oil and the vinegar. Season well with salt and pepper. Soak the cocktail sticks in water for 10 minutes before use, to prevent them from burning.

3 With a teaspoon, fill the squid with the stuffing mixture. Secure the open ends with the wooden cocktail sticks.

4 Brush the squid with the remaining oil and cook over a medium-hot barbecue for 4–5 minutes, turning often. Sprinkle with lemon juice and extra basil to serve.

Salmon with Tropical Fruit Salsa

Fresh salmon needs little adornment but does combine very well with the exotic flavours in this colourful salsa.

Serves 4

4 salmon steaks or fillets, about 175 g/6 oz each
finely grated rind and juice of 1 lime
1 small, ripe mango
1 small, ripe paw-paw
1 red chilli
45 ml/3 tbsp chopped fresh coriander
salt and freshly ground black pepper

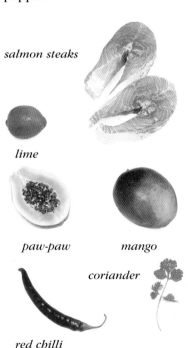

salmon steaks

lime

paw-paw

mango

coriander

red chilli

COOK'S TIP

If fresh red chillies are not available, use about 2.5 ml/ 1/2 tsp of chilli paste from a jar, or add a dash of chilli sauce.

1 Place the salmon in a wide dish and sprinkle over half the lime rind and juice. Season with salt and pepper.

2 Cut the mango in half, cutting either side of the stone, and then remove the stone. Finely chop the mango flesh.

3 Halve the paw-paw, scoop out the seeds and remove the peel: chop the flesh finely.

4 Cut the chilli in half lengthways. For a milder flavour, remove the seeds, or leave the seeds in to make the salsa hot and spicy. Finely chop the chilli.

5 Combine the mango, paw-paw, chilli and coriander in a bowl and stir in the remaining lime rind and juice. Season to taste with salt and pepper.

6 Cook the salmon on a hot barbecue for 5–8 minutes, turning once. Serve with the salsa.

Monkfish with Peppered Citrus Marinade

Monkfish is a firm, meaty fish that cooks well on the barbecue and keeps its shape well. Serve with a green salad.

Serves 4

2 monkfish tails, about 350 g/
  12 oz each
1 lime
1 lemon
2 oranges
handful of fresh thyme sprigs
15 ml/1 tbsp mixed
  peppercorns, roughly crushed
30 ml/2 tbsp olive oil
salt and freshly ground black
  pepper

monkfish tails

lemon

lime

oranges

olive oil

thyme sprigs

mixed peppercorns

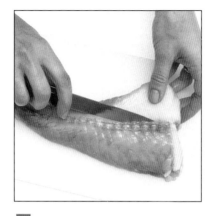

1 Remove any skin from the monkfish tails. Cut carefully down one side of the backbone, sliding the knife between the bone and flesh, to remove the fillet on one side. You can ask your fishmonger to do this for you.

2 Turn the fish and repeat on the other side, to remove the second fillet. Repeat on the second tail. Lay the four fillets out flat

3 Cut two slices from each of the citrus fruits and arrange them over two of the fillets. Add a few sprigs of thyme and sprinkle with salt and pepper. Finely grate the rind from the remaining fruit and sprinkle it over the fish.

VARIATION

You can also use this marinade for monkfish kebabs.

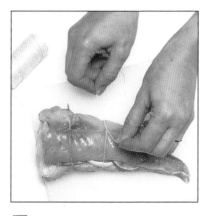

4 Lay the other two fillets on top and tie them firmly at intervals, with fine cotton string, to hold them in shape. Place in a wide dish.

5 Squeeze the juice from the citrus fruits and mix it with the oil and more salt and pepper. Spoon over the fish. Cover and leave to marinate for about an hour, turning occasionally and spooning the marinade over it.

6 Drain the monkfish, reserving the marinade, and sprinkle with the crushed peppercorns. Cook on a medium-hot barbecue for 15–20 minutes, basting it with the marinade and turning it occasionally, until it's evenly cooked.

Sardines with Warm Herb Salsa

Plain grilling is the very best way to cook fresh sardines; served with this luscious herb salsa the only other essential item is fresh, crusty bread, to mop up the tasty juices.

Serves 4

12–16 fresh sardines
oil for brushing
juice of 1 lemon

FOR THE SALSA
15 ml/1 tbsp butter
4 spring onions, chopped
1 garlic clove, finely chopped
30 ml/2 tbsp finely chopped
    fresh parsley
30 ml/2 tbsp finely snipped
    fresh chives
30 ml/2 tbsp finely chopped
    fresh basil
30 ml/2 tbsp green olive paste
10 ml/2 tsp balsamic vinegar
rind of 1 lemon
salt and freshly ground black
    pepper

sardines
butter
green olive paste
balsamic vinegar
lemon
spring onions
parsley
basil
chives

1 To clean the sardines, use small scissors to slit them along the belly and pull out the innards. Wipe the fish with kitchen paper and then arrange on a grill rack.

2 Melt the butter and gently sauté the spring onions and garlic for about 2 minutes, shaking the pan occasionally, until softened but not browned.

3 Add the lemon rind and remaining ingredients and keep warm on the edge of the barbecue. Do not allow to boil.

4 Brush the sardines lightly with oil and sprinkle with lemon juice, salt and pepper. Cook for about 2 minutes on each side, over a moderate heat. Serve with the warm salsa and crusty bread.

Spiced Fish Baked Thai-style

Banana leaves make a perfect, natural wrapping for barbecued foods, but if they are not available, you can use foil instead.

Serves 4

4 red snapper or mullet, about
    350 g/12 oz each
banana leaves
1 lime
1 garlic clove, thinly sliced
2 spring onions, thinly sliced
30 ml/2 tbsp Thai red curry
    paste
60 ml/4 tbsp coconut milk

red snapper

banana leaves

lime

garlic

spring onions   *coconut milk*

Thai red curry paste

COOK'S TIP

A large, whole fish can also be cooked this way. A rough guide for cooking whole fish is to allow about 10 minutes per 2.5 cm/1 in thickness.

1 Clean the fish, removing the scales, and then cut several deep slashes in the side of each. Place each fish on a layer of banana leaves.

2 Thinly slice half the lime and tuck the slices into the slashes in the fish, with slivers of garlic. Scatter the spring onions over the fish.

3 Grate the rind and squeeze the juice from the remaining half-lime and mix with the curry paste and coconut milk. Spoon over the fish.

4 Wrap the leaves over the fish, to enclose them completely. Tie firmly with string and cook on a medium-hot barbecue for about 15–20 minutes, turning occasionally.

Char-grilled Tuna with Fiery Pepper Purée

Tuna is an oily fish that grills well and is meaty enough to combine successfully with quite strong flavours – even hot chilli, as in this red pepper purée, which is excellent served with fresh, crusty bread.

COOK'S TIP
The pepper purée can be made in advance, by cooking the peppers and onion under a hot grill; keep it in the fridge until you cook the fish.

Serves 4

4 tuna steaks, about 175 g/6 oz
  each
finely grated rind and juice of
  1 lime
30 ml/2 tbsp olive oil
salt and freshly ground black
  pepper

FOR THE PEPPER PURÉE
2 red peppers, seeded and
  halved
1 small onion
2 garlic cloves, crushed
2 red chillies
1 slice white bread without
  crusts, diced
45 ml/3 tbsp olive oil, plus extra
  for brushing
lime wedges, to serve

lime

olive oil

red peppers   *garlic*

red chillies

tuna steaks

onion   *diced white bread*

1 Trim any skin from the tuna and place the steaks in one layer in a wide dish. Sprinkle over the lime rind and juice, oil, salt and pepper. Cover and refrigerate until required.

2 To make the pepper purée, brush the pepper halves with a little oil and cook them, skin-side down, on a hot barbecue, until the skin is blackened. Place the onion in its skin on the barbecue and cook until browned, turning it occasionally.

3 Leave to cool slightly, covered with a clean cloth, and then remove the skins from the peppers and the onion.

4 Place the peppers, onion, garlic, chillies, bread and oil in a food processor. Process until smooth. Add salt to taste.

5 Lift the tuna steaks from the marinade and cook them on a hot barbecue for 8–10 minutes, turning once, until golden brown. Serve with the pepper purée and crusty bread.

Barbecued Scallops with Lime Butter

Fresh scallops are quick to cook and ideal for barbecues. This recipe combines them simply with lime and fennel.

Serves 4

1 head fennel
2 limes
12 large scallops, cleaned
1 egg yolk
90 ml/6 tbsp melted butter
oil for brushing
salt and freshly ground black
   pepper

fennel

egg

limes

melted butter

scallops

1 Trim any feathery leaves from the fennel and reserve them. Slice the rest lengthways into thin wedges.

2 Cut one lime into wedges. Finely grate the rind and squeeze the juice of the other lime and toss half the juice and rind onto the scallops. Season well.

3 Place the egg yolk and remaining lime rind and juice in a bowl and whisk hard until pale and smooth.

4 Gradually whisk in the melted butter and continue whisking until thick and smooth. Finely chop the reserved fennel leaves and stir them in, with seasoning to taste.

5 Brush the fennel wedges with oil and cook them on a hot barbecue for 3–4 minutes, turning once.

6 Add the scallops and cook for a further 3–4 minutes, turning once. Serve with the lime and fennel butter and the lime wedges.

COOK'S TIP
If the scallops are small, it may be easier to thread them on to flat skewers, to make turning them easier.

Fish Parcels

Sea bass is good for this recipe, but you could also use small whole trout, or white fish fillet such as cod or haddock.

Serves 4

4 pieces sea bass fillet or 4
  whole small sea bass, about
  450 g/1 lb each
oil for brushing
2 shallots, thinly sliced
1 garlic clove, chopped
15 ml/1 tbsp capers
6 sun-dried tomatoes, finely
  chopped
4 black olives, pitted and thinly
  sliced
grated rind and juice of
  1 lemon
5 ml/1 tsp paprika
salt and freshly ground black
  pepper

COOK'S TIP

These parcels can also be baked in the oven: place them on a baking sheet and cook at 200°C/400°F/Gas Mark 6 for 15–20 minutes.

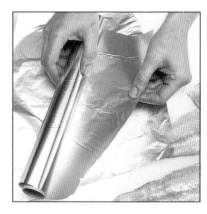

1 Clean the fish if whole. Cut four large squares of double-thickness foil, large enough to enclose the fish; brush with a little oil.

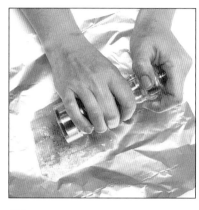

2 Place a piece of fish in the centre of each piece of foil and season well with salt and pepper.

3 Scatter over the shallots, garlic, capers, tomatoes, olives and grated lemon rind. Sprinkle with the lemon juice and paprika.

paprika

shallots

lemon

garlic

sun-dried tomatoes

capers

black olives

sea bass fillets

4 Fold the foil over to enclose the fish loosely, sealing the edges firmly so none of the juices can escape. Place on a moderately-hot barbecue and cook for 8–10 minutes. Then open up the tops of the parcels and serve.

Potato Skewers with Mustard Dip

Potatoes cooked on the barbecue have a tasty flavour and crisp skin. These are served with a thick, garlic-rich dip.

Serves 4

FOR THE DIP
4 garlic cloves, crushed
2 egg yolks
30 ml/2 tbsp lemon juice
300 ml/½ pint/1¼ cups extra-virgin olive oil
10 ml/2 tsp whole-grain mustard
salt and freshly ground black pepper

FOR THE POTATOES
1 kg/2 lb small new potatoes
200 g/7 oz/2 cups shallots, halved
30 ml/2 tbsp olive oil
15 ml/1 tbsp sea salt

lemon *new potatoes*

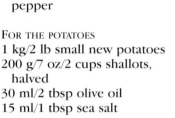
extra-virgin olive oil

shallots *garlic*

egg yolk

whole-grain mustard

1 To make the dip, place the garlic, egg yolks and lemon juice in a blender or food processor and process for a few seconds until smooth.

2 Keep the motor running and add the oil very gradually, pouring it in a thin stream, until the mixture forms a thick, glossy cream. Add the mustard and season with salt and pepper.

3 Par-boil the potatoes in boiling water for 5 minutes. Drain well and then thread them on to metal skewers, with the shallots.

4 Brush with oil and sprinkle with sea salt. Cook for 10–12 minutes over a hot barbecue, turning occasionally, until tender. Serve with the dip.

Roasted Garlic Toasts

A delicious starter or accompaniment to meat or vegetable dishes.

Serves 4

2 whole garlic heads
extra-virgin olive oil
fresh rosemary sprigs
ciabatta loaf or thick baguette
chopped fresh rosemary
salt and freshly ground black
   pepper

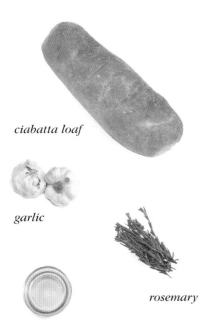

ciabatta loaf

garlic

rosemary

extra-virgin olive oil

1 Slice the tops from the heads of garlic, with a sharp knife.

2 Brush with oil, and then wrap in foil, with a few sprigs of rosemary. Cook on a medium–hot barbecue for 25–30 minutes, turning occasionally, until soft.

3 Slice the bread and brush generously with oil. Toast on the barbecue until golden, turning once.

4 Squeeze the garlic cloves from their skins on to the toasts; then sprinkle the toasts with chopped fresh rosemary and little extra olive oil, with salt and pepper to taste.

COOK'S TIP

Roast a few aubergine, pepper or onion slices, to spread over the toasts, for variety.

Red Bean and Mushroom Burgers

Vegetarians, vegans and even meat-eaters can all enjoy these healthy, low-fat veggie burgers. With salad, pitta bread and Greek-style yogurt, they make a substantial meal.

COOK'S TIP
These burgers are not quite as firm as meat burgers, so handle them gently on the barbecue.

Serves 4

15 ml/1 tbsp olive oil
1 small onion, finely chopped
1 garlic clove, crushed
5 ml/1 tsp ground cumin
5 ml/1 tsp ground coriander
2.5 ml/$\frac{1}{2}$ tsp ground turmeric
115 g/4 oz/1$\frac{1}{2}$ cups finely chopped mushrooms
400 g/14 oz can red kidney beans
30 ml/2 tbsp chopped fresh coriander
wholemeal flour (optional)
olive oil for brushing
salt and black pepper
Greek-style yogurt, to serve

mushrooms

wholemeal flour

red kidney beans

onion

garlic

olive oil

cumin

coriander

turmeric

ground coriander

1 Heat the oil in a wide pan and fry the onion and garlic over a moderate heat, stirring, until softened. Add the spices and cook for a further minute, stirring continuously.

2 Add the mushrooms and cook, stirring, until softened and dry. Remove from the heat.

3 Drain the beans thoroughly and then mash them with a fork.

4 Stir into the pan, with the fresh coriander, mixing thoroughly. Season well with salt and pepper.

5 Using floured hands, form the mixture into four flat burger shapes. If the mixture is too sticky to handle, mix in a little flour.

6 Brush the burgers with oil and cook on a hot barbecue for 8–10 minutes, turning once, until golden brown. Serve with a spoonful of yogurt and a crisp green salad.

Aubergine, Tomato and Feta Rolls

Grilled aubergines wrapped around tangy feta cheese, flavoured with basil and sun-dried tomatoes make a wonderful combination of sunshine flavours.

Serves 4

2 large aubergines
olive oil
10–12 sun-dried tomatoes in oil, drained
handful of large, fresh basil leaves
150 g/5 oz feta cheese
salt and freshly ground black pepper

olive oil

aubergines

feta cheese

sun-dried tomatoes in oil
basil

COOK'S TIP

Vegetarians or vegans could use tofu in place of the feta cheese. For extra flavour, sprinkle the tofu with a little soy sauce before wrapping.

1 Slice the aubergines lengthways into 5 mm/¼ in thick slices. Sprinkle with salt and layer in a colander. Leave to drain for about 30 minutes.

2 Rinse the aubergines in cold water and dry well. Brush with oil on both sides and grill on a hot barbecue for 2–3 minutes, turning once, until golden brown and softened.

3 Arrange the sun-dried tomatoes over one end of each aubergine slice and top with the basil leaves. Cut the feta into short sticks and place on top. Season with salt and pepper.

4 Roll the aubergine slices around to enclose the filling. Cook on the barbecue for a further 2–3 minutes, until hot. Serve with ciabatta bread.

Brie Parcels with Almonds

A sophisticated starter or light main course, served with crusty bread.

Serves 4

4 large vine leaves, preservéd in
  brine
200 g/7 oz piece Brie cheese
30 ml/2 tbsp chopped fresh
  chives
30 ml/2 tbsp ground almonds
5 ml/1 tsp crushed black
  peppercorns
15 ml/1 tbsp olive oil
flaked almonds

vine leaves

Brie cheese

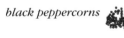

black peppercorns

chives

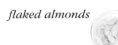

flaked almonds

olive oil

ground almonds

1 Rinse the vine leaves thoroughly in cold water and dry them well. Spread the leaves out on a board.

2 Cut the Brie into four chunks and place each chunk on a vine leaf.

3 Mix together the chives, ground almonds, peppercorns and oil; then place a spoonful on top of each piece of cheese. Sprinkle with flaked almonds.

4 Fold the vine leaves over, to enclose the cheese completely. Brush with oil and cook on a hot barbecue for 3–4 minutes, until the cheese is hot and melting. Serve immediately.

Grilled Mediterranean Vegetables with Marbled Yogurt Pesto

Char-grilled summer vegetables – a meal on its own, or delicious served as an accompaniment to grilled meats and fish.

COOK'S TIP
Baby vegetables make excellent candidates for grilling whole, so look out for baby aubergines and peppers, in particular. There's no need to salt the aubergines, if they're small.

Serves 4

2 small aubergines
2 large courgettes
1 red pepper
1 yellow pepper
1 fennel bulb
1 red onion
olive oil for brushing

FOR THE SAUCE
150 ml/¼ pint/⅔ cup Greek-style yogurt
45 ml/3 tbsp pesto
salt and freshly ground black pepper

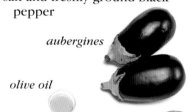

aubergines

olive oil

pesto

courgettes

Greek-style yogurt

fennel

red pepper

red onion   *yellow pepper*

1 Cut the aubergines into 1 cm/½ in thick slices. Sprinkle with salt and leave to drain for about 30 minutes. Rinse and dry well.

2 Cut the courgettes in half lengthways. Cut the peppers in half, remove the seeds but leave the stalk on.

3 Slice the fennel and the onion into thick wedges.

4 Stir the yogurt and pesto lightly together, to make a marbled sauce. Spoon into a serving bowl.

5 Arrange the vegetables on the hot barbecue, brush with oil and sprinkle with salt and pepper.

6 Cook the vegetables until golden brown and tender, turning occasionally. The aubergines and peppers will take 6–8 minutes to cook, the courgettes, onion and fennel 4–5 minutes. Serve with the marbled pesto sauce.

Herb Polenta with Grilled Tomatoes

Golden polenta with fresh summer herbs and sweet grilled tomatoes.

COOK'S TIP

Any mixture of fresh herbs can be used, or try using just basil or chives alone, for a really distinctive flavour.

Serves 4

750 litres/1¼ pints/3⅔ cups
  stock or water
5 ml/1 tsp salt
175 g/6 oz/1 cup polenta
25 g/1 oz/2 tbsp butter
75 ml/5 tbsp mixed chopped
  fresh parsley, chives and basil,
  plus extra, to garnish
olive oil for brushing
4 large plum or beef tomatoes,
  halved
salt and freshly ground black
  pepper

stock

plum tomatoes

polenta

butter

thyme

chives

parsley

basil

1 Prepare the polenta in advance: place the water or stock in a pan, with the salt, and bring to the boil. Reduce the heat and stir in the polenta.

2 Stir constantly over a moderate heat for 5 minutes, until the polenta begins to thicken and come away from the sides of the pan.

3 Remove from the heat and stir in the butter, herbs and black pepper.

4 Tip the mixture into a wide, greased tin or dish and spread it out evenly. Leave until completely cool and set.

5 Turn out the polenta and cut it into squares or stamp out rounds with a large biscuit cutter. Brush with oil.

6 Brush the tomatoes with oil and sprinkle with salt and pepper. Cook the tomatoes and polenta on a medium hot barbecue for 5 minutes, turning once. Serve garnished with fresh herbs.

Barbecued Goat's Cheese Pizza

Pizzas cooked on the barbecue have a beautifully crisp and golden base.

Serves 4

150 g/5 oz packet pizza-base mix
olive oil for brushing
150 ml/¼ pint/⅔ cup passata
30 ml/2 tbsp red pesto sauce
1 small red onion, thinly sliced
8 cherry tomatoes, halved
115 g/4 oz firm goat's cheese, thinly sliced
handful chopped fresh basil leaves
salt and freshly ground black pepper

passata

pizza-base mix

goat's cheese

red pesto sauce

red onion

basil

cherry tomatoes

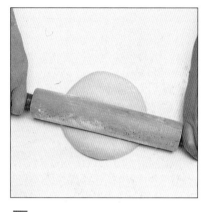

1 Make up the pizza dough, according to packet directions. Roll out to a round of about 25 cm/10 in diameter.

2 Brush the dough with oil and place, oiled-side down, on a medium-hot barbecue. Cook for about 6–8 minutes, until firm and golden underneath.

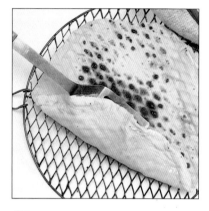

3 Brush the top of the dough with oil and turn the dough over, to cook the other side.

4 Mix together the passata and pesto sauce and quickly spread over the cooked side of the pizza, to within about 1 cm/½ in of the edge.

5 Arrange the onion, tomatoes and cheese slices on top and sprinkle with salt and pepper.

6 Cook the pizza for a further 8–10 minutes, or until the dough is golden brown and crisp. Sprinkle with chopped basil and serve.

Golden Vegetable Parcels with Flowery Butter

Nasturtium leaves and flowers have a distinctive peppery flavour, and make a pretty addition to summer dishes.

Serves 4

200 g/7 oz baby carrots
250 g/9 oz yellow patty-pan
  squash or yellow courgettes
115 g/4 oz baby sweetcorn
1 onion, thinly sliced
50 g/2 oz/4 tbsp butter
finely grated rind ½ lemon
6 young nasturtium leaves
4–8 nasturtium flowers
salt and freshly ground black
  pepper

butter

baby carrots

lemon

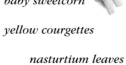
baby sweetcorn

yellow courgettes

nasturtium leaves

onion   *nasturtium flowers*

COOK'S TIP
Other edible flowers, such as marigold petals, or purple chive flowers, can be used instead of the nasturtiums. When cooking with flowers, always ensure that they really are edible ones.

1 Trim the vegetables and leave them whole unless they are too large – if necessary, cut them in even-sized pieces.

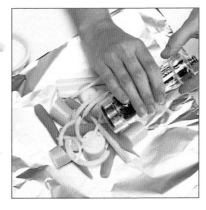
2 Divide the vegetables between four double-thickness squares of foil and season with salt and pepper.

3 Mix the butter with the lemon rind. Roughly chop the nasturtium leaves and add to the butter. Place a spoonful of the butter on each pile of vegetables.

4 Fold over the foil and seal the edges to make a neat parcel. Cook on a medium-hot barbecue for 25–30 minutes until the vegetables are tender. Open the parcels and top each with one or two nasturtium flowers. Serve immediately.

Grilled Corn with Ginger Hazelnut Butter

Corn cooked on the barbecue is deliciously nutty and sweet. But take care to cook it slowly, so as not to dry it out.

Serves 4

15 ml/1 tbsp olive oil
45 ml/3 tbsp finely chopped hazelnuts
2.5 cm/1 in piece fresh root ginger, finely chopped
75 g/3 oz/6 tbsp butter
salt and freshly ground black pepper
4 corn cobs

corn cobs

fresh root ginger

hazelnuts

olive oil

butter

1 Heat the oil in a small pan and gently fry the hazelnuts, stirring, until they are golden brown.

2 Remove from the heat, cool slightly, and then stir in the ginger.

3 Mix in the butter, with salt and pepper to taste.

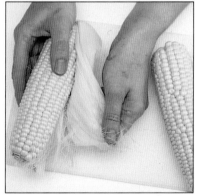

4 Remove the husks and silks from the corn cobs and grill on a hot barbecue, turning frequently, for 20–25 minutes, until golden brown and tender. Serve with the ginger hazelnut butter.

COOK'S TIP

If you prefer, the corn cobs can be wrapped in buttered foil and cooked in the coals of the fire – the cooking time should be reduced to 15–20 minutes.

Baked Squash with Parmesan

Almost all types of squash are suitable for barbecue cooking, and they are extremely easy to cook in this way.

Serves 4

2 acorn or butternut squash,
 about 450 g/1 lb each
15 ml/1 tbsp olive oil
50 g/2 oz/4 tbsp butter, melted
75 g/3 oz/1 cup grated fresh
 Parmesan cheese
2.5 ml/½ tsp grated nutmeg
60 ml/4 tbsp pine nuts, toasted
salt and freshly ground black
 pepper

butter

squash

olive oil

Parmesan cheese

pine nuts

nutmeg

COOK'S TIP
Spaghetti squash can also be cooked in this way. Just scoop out the spaghetti-like strands and toss them with the butter and Parmesan.

1 Cut the squash in half and scoop out the seeds.

2 Brush the cut surface with oil and sprinkle with salt and pepper.

3 Wrap the squash in foil and place in the embers of the fire. Turn occasionally, making sure the parcels cook evenly. Cook for 25–30 minutes, until tender.

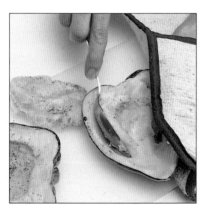

4 Unwrap the squash and scoop out the flesh, leaving the skin intact.

5 Dice the flesh and then stir in the melted butter. Add the Parmesan cheese, pine nuts, salt and pepper. Toss well to mix evenly.

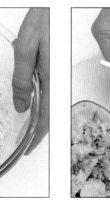

6 Spoon the mixture back into the squash shells and sprinkle with grated nutmeg before serving.

DESSERTS

Char-grilled Apples on Cinnamon Toasts

This simple, scrumptious dessert is best made with an enriched bread such as brioche, but any light, sweet bread will do.

Serves 4

4 sweet dessert apples
juice of ½ lemon
4 individual brioches or muffins
60 ml/4 tbsp melted butter
30 ml/2 tbsp golden caster
  sugar
5 ml/1 tsp ground cinnamon
cream or Greek-style yogurt, to
  serve

sweet dessert apples

golden caster sugar

lemon

brioches

melted butter

ground cinnamon

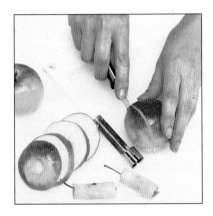

1 Core the apples and then cut them horizontally in 3–4 thick slices. Sprinkle with lemon juice.

2 Cut the brioches or muffins into thick slices. Brush with melted butter on both sides.

3 Mix together the sugar and cinnamon.

4 Place the apple and brioche slices on the hot barbecue and cook them for 3–4 minutes, turning once, until they are beginning to turn golden brown.

5 Sprinkle half the cinnamon sugar over the apple slices and toasts and cook for a further minute, until they are a rich golden brown.

6 To serve, arrange the apple slices over the toasts and sprinkle them with the remaining cinnamon sugar. Serve hot, with cream or yogurt.

Pineapple Wedges with Rum Butter Glaze

Fresh pineapple is even more full of flavour when grilled; this spiced rum glaze makes it into a very special dessert.

Serves 4

1 medium pineapple
30 ml/2 tbsp dark muscovado
   sugar
5 ml/1 tsp ground ginger
60 ml/4 tbsp melted butter
30 ml/2 tbsp dark rum

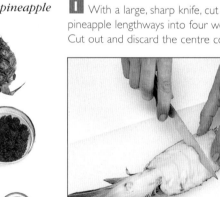

pineapple

melted butter

dark muscovado sugar

ground ginger   *dark rum*

1 With a large, sharp knife, cut the pineapple lengthways into four wedges. Cut out and discard the centre core.

2 Cut between the flesh and skin, to release the flesh, but leave the skin in place. Slice the flesh across, into chunks.

COOK'S TIP

For an easier version, simply cut off the skin and then slice the whole pineapple into thick slices and cook as above.

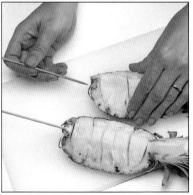

3 Push a bamboo skewer lengthways through each wedge and into the stalk, to hold the chunks in place.

4 Mix together the sugar, ginger, melted butter and rum and brush over the pineapple. Cook the wedges on a hot barbecue for 3–4 minutes; pour the remaining glaze over the top and serve.

Baked Bananas with Spicy Vanilla Butter

Baked bananas are a must for the barbecue – they're so easy because they bake in their own skins and need no preparation at all. A flavoured butter melting over them adds richness. Children may simply prefer melted chocolate, jam or honey over their bananas.

Serves 4

4 bananas
6 green cardamom pods
1 vanilla pod
finely grated rind of 1 small
   orange
30 ml/2 tbsp brandy or orange
   juice
60 ml/4 tbsp light muscovado
   sugar
45 ml/3 tbsp butter
crème fraîche or Greek-style
   yogurt, to serve

brandy
butter
orange
bananas
green cardamom pods
vanilla pod
light muscovado sugar

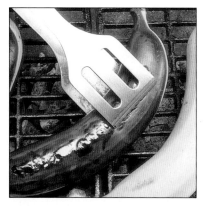

1 Place the bananas, in their skins, on the hot barbecue and leave for 6–8 minutes, turning occasionally, until they are turning brownish-black.

2 Meanwhile, split the cardamom pods and remove the seeds. Crush lightly in a pestle and mortar.

3 Split the vanilla pod lengthways and scrape out the tiny seeds. Mix with the cardamom seeds, orange rind, brandy or juice, sugar and butter, into a thick paste.

4 Slit the skin of each banana, open out slightly and spoon in a little of the paste. Serve with a spoonful of crème fraîche or Greek-style yogurt.

Oranges in Maple and Cointreau Syrup

This is one of the most delicious ways to eat an orange, and a luxurious way to round off a barbecue party.

Serves 4

20 ml/4 tsp butter, plus extra, melted, for brushing
4 medium-size oranges
30 ml/2 tbsp maple syrup
30 ml/2 tbsp Cointreau or Grand Marnier liqueur
crème fraîche or fromage frais, to serve

Cointreau liqueur

oranges

butter

maple syrup

1 Cut four double-thickness squares of foil, large enough to wrap the oranges. Brush the centre of each with melted butter.

2 Remove some shreds of orange rind, to decorate. Blanch them, dry them and set them aside. Peel the oranges, removing all the white pith and peel and catching the juice in a bowl.

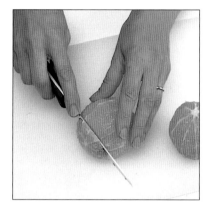

3 Slice the oranges crossways into several thick slices. Reassemble them and place each orange on a square of foil.

4 Tuck the foil up around the oranges, to keep them in shape, leaving the foil open at the top.

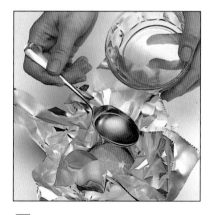

5 Mix together the reserved orange juice, maple syrup and liqueur and spoon the mixture over the oranges.

6 Add a dab of butter to each parcel and fold over the foil, to seal in the juices. Place the parcels on a hot barbecue for 10–12 minutes, until hot. Serve with crème fraîche or fromage frais, topped with shreds of orange rind.

COOK'S TIP
For a children's or alcohol-free version, omit the liqueur.

Nectarines with Marzipan and Mascarpone

A luscious dessert that no one can resist – dieters may like to use low-fat soft cheese or ricotta instead of mascarpone.

Serves 4

4 firm, ripe nectarines or
  peaches
75 g/3 oz marzipan
75 g/3 oz/5 tbsp mascarpone
  cheese
3 macaroon biscuits, crushed

mascarpone cheese

nectarines

marzipan

macaroon biscuits

COOK'S TIP

Either peaches or nectarines can be used for this recipe. If the stone does not pull out easily when you halve the fruit, use a small, sharp knife to cut around it.

1 Cut the nectarines or peaches in half, removing the stones.

2 Cut the marzipan into eight pieces and press one piece into the stone cavity of each nectarine half.

3 Spoon the mascarpone on top. Sprinkle the crushed macaroons over the mascarpone.

4 Place the half-fruits on a hot barbecue for 3–5 minutes, until they are hot and the mascarpone starts to melt.

Barbecued Strawberry Croissants

A deliciously simple, sinful dessert, which is like eating warm cream cakes!

Serves 4

4 croissants
115 g/4 oz/½ cup ricotta cheese
115 g/4 oz/½ cup strawberry
 conserve or jam

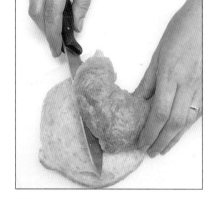

1 Split the croissants in half and open them out on a board.

croissants

ricotta cheese

strawberry conserve

2 Spread the bottom half of each croissant with ricotta cheese.

3 Top with a generous spoonful of strawberry conserve and replace the top half of the croissant.

4 Place the croissants on a hot barbecue and cook for 2–3 minutes, turning once.

COOK'S TIP

As an alternative to croissants, try fresh scones or muffins, toasted on the barbecue.

Griddle Cakes with Mulled Plums

Delectably light little pancakes, with a rich, spicy plum sauce.

Serves 6

500 g/1¼ lb red plums
90 ml/6 tbsp light muscovado
    sugar
1 cinnamon stick
2 whole cloves
1 piece star anise
90 ml/6 tbsp apple juice

For the griddle cakes
50 g/2 oz/½ cup plain flour
10 ml/2 tsp baking powder
pinch of salt
50 g/2 oz/½ cup fine cornmeal
30 ml/2 tbsp light muscovado
    sugar
1 egg, beaten
300 ml/½ pint/1¼ cups milk
30 ml/2 tbsp corn oil
cream or Greek-style yogurt, to
    serve

baking powder *light muscovado sugar*

fine cornmeal

plain flour *star anise*

red plums

egg *cinnamon stick* *cloves*

apple juice *corn oil*

1 Halve, stone and quarter the plums. Place them in a pan, with the sugar, spices and apple juice.

COOK'S TIP

If you prefer, make the griddle cakes in advance, on the hob, and then simply heat them for a few seconds on the barbecue, to serve with the plums.

2 Place on a hot barbecue or hob and bring to the boil. Reduce the heat, cover the pan and simmer gently for 8–10 minutes, stirring occasionally, until the plums are soft. Remove the spices and keep the plums warm.

3 For the griddle cakes, sift the flour, baking powder and salt into a large bowl and stir in the cornmeal and sugar.

4 Make a well in the centre and add the egg; gradually beat in the milk. Beat thoroughly with a whisk or wooden spoon to form a smooth batter. Beat in half the oil.

5 Heat a griddle or a heavy frying-pan on a hot barbecue until it's very hot. Brush it with the remaining oil and then drop tablespoons of batter on to it, allowing them to spread. Cook the griddle cakes for about a minute, until bubbles start to appear on the surface and the underside is golden.

6 Turn the cakes over with a palette knife and cook the other side for a further minute, or until golden. Serve hot from the griddle with a spoonful of mulled plums and cream or yogurt.

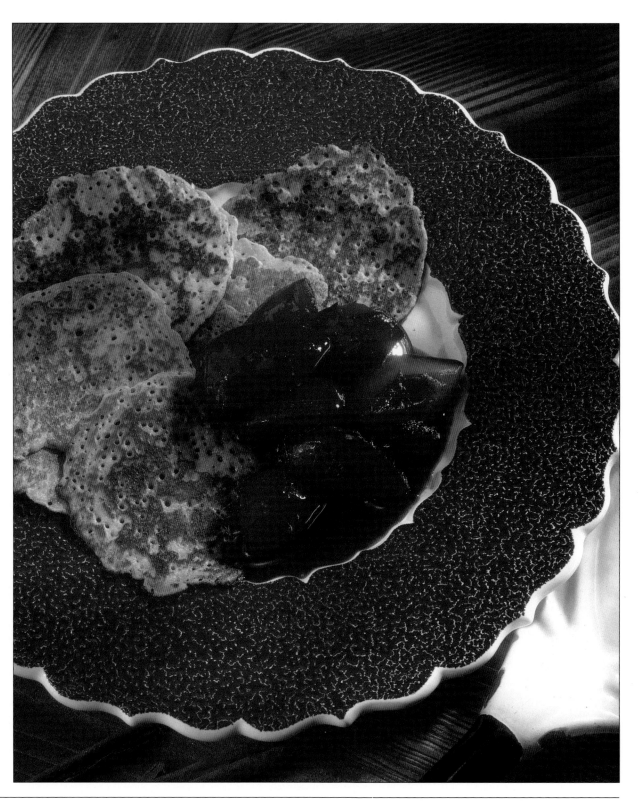

Fruit Kebabs with Chocolate and Marshmallow Fondue

Children love these treats – and with supervision they can help to make them.

Serves 4

2 bananas
2 kiwi fruit
12 strawberries
15 ml/1 tbsp melted butter
15 ml/1 tbsp lemon juice
5 ml/1 tsp ground cinnamon

FOR THE FONDUE
225 g/8 oz plain chocolate
100 ml/4 fl oz/½ cup single
  cream
8 marshmallows
2.5 ml/½ tsp vanilla essence

plain chocolate

vanilla essence

bananas

lemon juice

ground cinnamon

melted butter

single cream

marshmallows

kiwi fruit

strawberries

1 Peel the bananas and cut each into six thick chunks. Peel the kiwi fruit thinly and quarter them. Thread the bananas, kiwi fruit and strawberries on to four wooden or bamboo skewers.

2 Mix together the butter, lemon juice and cinnamon and brush the mixture over the fruits.

3 For the fondue, place the chocolate, cream and marshmallows in a small pan and heat gently on the barbecue, without boiling, stirring until the mixture has melted and is smooth.

4 Cook the kebabs on the barbecue for 2–3 minutes, turning once, or until golden. Stir the vanilla essence into the fondue and serve it with the kebabs.

Spiced Pear and Blueberry Parcels

This combination makes a delicious dessert for a summer's evening.

Serves 4

4 firm, ripe pears
30 ml/2 tbsp lemon juice
15 ml/1 tbsp melted butter
150 g/5 oz/1¼ cups blueberries
60 ml/4 tbsp light muscovado
  sugar
freshly ground black pepper

pears

blueberries

light muscovado sugar

black peppercorns

melted butter

lemon

COOK'S TIP

If you wish to assemble the dessert in advance, place a layer of greaseproof paper inside the parcel, because the acid in the lemon juice may react with the foil and taint the flavour.

1 Peel the pears thinly. Cut them in half lengthways. Scoop out the core from each half, with a teaspoon and a sharp knife.

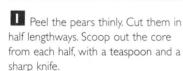

2 Brush the pears with lemon juice, to prevent them from browning.

3 Cut four squares of double-thickness foil, large enough to wrap the pears; brush them with melted butter. Place two pear-halves on each, cut-side upwards. Gather the foil up around them, to hold them level.

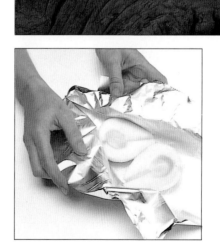

4 Mix the blueberries and sugar together and spoon them on top of the pears. Sprinkle with black pepper. Wrap the foil over and cook on a fairly hot barbecue, for 20–25 minutes.

A

Apples:
    char-grilled apples on
        cinnamon toasts, 84
Aubergine, tomato and feta
    rolls, 72

B

Bacon:
    bacon kofta kabobs and
        salad, 24
    char-grilled sausages with
        prunes and bacon, 30
    mixed grill skewers with
        horseradish butter, 36
Bananas:
    baked bananas with spicy
        vanilla butter, 87
Barbecue cooking, timing guide
    14, 15
Basic barbecue marinade, 21
Beef:
    basic burgers, 18
    peppered steaks in beer and
        garlic, 39
    Stilton burger, 18
    Tex-Mex burgers in tortillas,
        26

C

Cheese:
    aubergine, tomato and feta
        rolls, 72
    barbecued goat's cheese
        pizza, 78
    Brie parcels with almonds,
        73
    chicken with herb and ricota
        stuffing, 43
    ham pizzettes with melted
        Brie and Mango, 32
    nectarines with marzipan and
        Mascarpone, 90
    Stilton burger,18
Chicken:
    baby chickens with lime and

chilli, 44
    blackened Cajun chicken and
        corn, 40
    chicken breasts cooked in
        spices and coconut, 48
    chicken wings Teriyaki-style,
        42
    chicken with herb and ricota
        stuffing 43
Cucumber relish, 19

D

Duck:
    apricot duck breasts with
        bean sprout salad, 46

F

Fire, lighting, 16
Fish:
    whole, preparing for grilling,
        17
Foil parcels, cooking in, 17
Fruit kebabs with chocolate and
    marshmallow fondue, 94
Fuel, types of, 10

G

Garlic:
    roasted garlic toasts, 69
Griddled cakes with mulled
    plums, 92

H

Ham pizzettes with melted Brie
    and mango, 32
Heat, controlling, 16
Herb marinade, 21
Honey citrus marinade, 21

K

Kidney beans:
    red bean and mushroom
        burgers, 70

L

Lamb:

barbecued lamb with potato
    slices, 28
minty lamb burgers with
    redcurrant chutney, 22
mixed grill skewers with
    horseradish butter, 36
racks of lamb with lavender
    balsamic marinade, 38

M

Mackerel kebabs with sweet
    pepper salad, 52
Marinades, 21
Marinating, 20
Monkfish with peppered citrus
    marinade, 58
Mushrooms
    red bean and mushroom
        burgers, 70

N

Nectarines with marzipan and
    Mascarpone, 90

O

Oranges in maple and
    Cointreau syrup, 88

P

Pears:
    spiced pear and blueberry
        parcels, 95
Peppers:
    char-grilled tuna with fiery
        pepper purée, 62
    mackerel kebabs with sweet
        pepper salad, 52
    turkey rolls with gazpacho
        sauce, 41
Pheasants with sage and lemon,
    50
Pineapple:
    pineapple wedge with rum
        butter glaze, 86
    pork and pineapple satay, 34

Polenta:
    herb polenta with grilled
        tomatoes, 76
Pork:
    five-spice rib-stickers, 31
    pork and pineapple satay, 34
Potatoes:
    barbecued lamb with potato
        slices, 28
    potato skewers with mustard
        dip, 68
Prawns:
    tiger prawn skewers with
        walnut pesto, 54
Prunes:
    char-grilled sausages with
        prunes and bacon, 30

Q

Quick barbecue relish, 19

R

Red snapper or mullet:
    spiced fish Thai-style, 61
Red-wine marinade, 21
Relishes, 19

S

Safety, 11
Salmon with tropical fruit salsa,
    56
Sardines with warm herb salsa,
    60
Sausages:
    char-grilled sausages with
        prunes and bacon, 30
    mixed grill skewers with
        horseradish butter, 36
Scallops:
    barbecued scallops with lime
        butter, 64
Sea bass:
    fish parcels, 66
Squash:
    baked squash with Parmesan,
        82

Squid:
    calimari with two-tomato
        stuffing, 55
Strawberries:
    barbecued strawberry
        croissants, 91
Sweetcorn:
    blackened Cajun chicken and
        corn, 40
    grilled corn with ginger
        hazelnut butter, 81

T

Tomatoes:
    aubergine, tomato and feta
        rolls, 72
    calimari with two-tomato
        stuffing, 55
    herb polenta with grilled
        tomatoes, 76
    tomato relish, 19
    turkey rolls with gazpacho
        sauce, 41
Tools and equipment, 12, 13
Tuna:
    char-grilled tuna with fiery
        pepper purée, 62
Turkey rolls with gazpacho
    sauce, 41
Types of barbecue, 8, 9

V

Vegetables:
    golden vegetable parcels
        with flowery butter, 80
    grilled Mediterranean
        vegetables with marbled
yogurt pesto, 74
Venison:
    juniper-spiced venison chops,
        49

Y

Yogurt spice marinade,: 21